PRAI

"For most of my life, I had ZERO control over my emotions, so my actions were driven by what I felt in the moment. If I'd had the research-backed strategies Dr. Shahana outlines for you in this book, I could have avoided a massive number of mistakes."

MEL ROBBINS, New York Times Bestselling Author,
Host of The Mel Robbins Podcast

"Dr. Shahana's vulnerability as a physician working in the space of mental health sets the tone for a courageous conversation when it comes to our mental health. *Feel Better* helps us build our emotional capacity—a bedrock for elevating our overall health and wellbeing."

ROBERT GLAZER, #1 WSJ and USA Today Bestselling
Author of *Elevate* and *Friday Forward*

"In clear language and by offering dozens of resonant examples, Dr. Shahana shows us how to address the emotional triggers that can undermine our mental and physical health. Her emphasis is firmly upon the how. She doesn't just advocate for self-awareness, she shows us how to practice it. She doesn't simply prescribe action, she shows us how we frame it to be most effective. Rooting her insights in her own experience with postpartum depression and her work with thousands of patients, both young and old, Dr. Shahana provides an invaluable guide for becoming our best and healthiest selves."

SALLY HELGESEN, Author of *Rising Together, How Women Rise*, and *The Female Advantage*

"*Feel Better* has an approach to mental and emotional health that is both relatable and refreshing. This is not just another mental health book, it is a testament and a tribute to the incredible grit, resilience, and courage faced by our young people today. Thank you, Dr. Shahana, for showcasing these incredible stories and, even more, our incredible youth!"

"With the humor of Mark Twain, the punch of Winston Churchill, and the eloquence of Shakespeare, Dr. Shahana has managed to take at least 25 of the self-help and Cognitive Behavioral Therapy books and condense them into one."

"*Feel Better* guides the reader through so many powerful tools to positively impact your overall well-being. It's a must read for your mental wellness!"

"*Feel Better* is a captivating blend of personal experiences and professional insights that touch the hearts of readers from all walks of life. Dr. Shahana's ability to translate her wisdom from the clinic to the stage is nothing short of inspiring. This book is an essential read for anyone seeking to find solace and inspiration in today's fast-paced world. I wholeheartedly endorse *Feel Better* as a must-read that deserves a place on every nightstand. Dr. Shahana's words resonate deeply, reminding us that, above all, we all share the universal desire to feel better."

"As a physician who deals with real people with very real mental health issues, Dr. Shahana's book is foundational for parents and youth to understand themselves in an increasingly complex world. Unlike the past when people could just learn through living, our current life needs us to acquire and teach skills that will help everyone 'Feel Better'. This concise yet in-depth book equips us to do just that."

DR. HOLDEN CHOW, Family Doctor and Site Director for UBC Family Practice Residency Program (Abbotsford-Mission Site)

"*Feel Better* is the instruction manual everyone can use and no one was given. It is part first aid kit and part insurance policy. With an easy-to-follow framework and exercises, *Feel Better* exceeds its hope that you become more emotionally healthy while boosting overall mental health. As much as I found my mind wandering into my own emotional corners and backroads, I was also absorbing simple exercises and strategies I could use as a husband, dad, and grandfather to help those I love better understand themselves and those around them."

SCOTT HOFFMAN, MBA, Investor, author of *The 10 Absolute Laws of Sales, Marketing and Customer Service*

FEEL BETTER

FEEL BETTER

HOW UNDERSTANDING YOUR EMOTIONAL PALETTE
CAN KEEP YOU FROM GETTING SWEPT AWAY

DR. SHAHANA ALIBHAI, MD

THRONE
PUBLISHING GROUP

Throne Publishing Group
ThronePG.com

First and foremost, this book is dedicated to my three beautiful boys: Eshaan, Ayaan, and Rahil. With you, I know what true joy looks like; without you, I would never have had the most important role in my life, which is a mother to you. May you always see yourselves as a person with potential.

To my husband, Khalid, I am the luckiest girl in the world to have you to walk alongside life with. I knew the minute I laid eyes on you that you would change my life forever. Thank you for being my best friend, my partner in life, and for believing in "Feel Better" before it was even an idea.

To my parents, my incredible sister Shabita, and my entire family: Thank you for your love, endless support and accepting me fully for who I am. I love you all more than words can say.

TABLE OF CONTENTS

Partial proceeds of every book sold will be donated back to community organizations to improve the mental and physical wellbeing of our youth.

FOREWORD

A few years ago, we hosted a fascinating guest on our Anxiety at Work Podcast. She was medical doctor who wasn't selling a book, didn't have a product to promote, and was one of the few people left in North America without a podcast. No, Shahana Alibhai came on our show as a busy working physician because she wanted to help people feel better about their mental health, nothing more.

We are the ones who told her she needed to write a book.

What Dr. Alibhai has to say is important. Today the importance of emotional intelligence has never been more pronounced. Yet, amidst the hustle of our modern lives, many of us find ourselves struggling to navigate the turbulent waters of our own emotions. Enter this groundbreaking book, a beacon of insight and guidance in the often-murky realm of emotional well-being.

At its core, *Feel Better* challenges the notion that emotional well-being is simply about feeling happier. Instead, it invites us to explore the depths of our emotional landscape with curiosity and intentionality, recognizing that true growth often arises from embracing even the most challenging aspects of our inner selves.

Dr. Alibhai acknowledges the inherent complexity of our emotional lives and offers practical strategies for regaining control of our attention and responses. Central to her message is the idea that we need not strive to control our emotions, but rather the attention we give them and the responses we choose to move forward with. Through mindfulness practices, cognitive-behavioral techniques, and the cultivation of self-compassion, we learn to navigate the ebb and flow of our emotions with grace and resilience.

We hope you know you are not alone on the journey toward emotional well-being. As you embark on this exploration of our inner landscape, together with others we can cultivate empathy and understanding for ourselves and those around us, forging deeper connections and more resilient communities along the way.

In these pages, you'll find not only a roadmap to greater emotional resilience but an invitation to embark on a process of self-discovery—one that promises to transform not only how we relate to our emotions but how we show up in the world. So, let's dive in, with open hearts and minds, ready to embrace the full spectrum of our humanity.

With gratitude,
ADRIAN GOSTICK AND ANTHONY GOSTICK
Bestselling Authors of *Anxiety at Work*

INTRODUCTION

I hated swimming as a kid. I remember the nauseating smell of chlorine as I entered the pool. Perhaps it wasn't the water but the thought of getting in and swimming that posed more of a problem. Front crawl was my nemesis. My effort was there, no one could argue with that. I spent my swim lessons panting and sputtering like a fish out of water, only to look up and find out the incredible strides I had made were only in my head. I'll never forget the feeling as our swim coach handed out report cards at the end of the season. My little envelope never seemed to bulge with the coveted swim badge given to all those who passed. The swim level Maroon—a color to this day I'm still not fond of—took me six attempts to complete before finally moving on to the next level.

It wasn't until a few years later that I discovered swim goggles. To be honest I always thought goggles were for the older kids or professional swimmers, not someone like me. The first time I realized I could have my eyes open underwater was a revelation. Not only could I see, but I found myself spending less time trying to wipe the chlorine out of my eyes and more time focusing on my breathing. I also knew where I was going. So instead of frantically trying to catch up with the class only to end up on the other side of the pool (which happened all the time!) I now found myself swimming along my lane.

The goggles didn't miraculously make me an incredible swimmer, they were just a vital tool I needed. They helped me see things more clearly and gave me a new perspective so the task of swimming became a little bit more manageable.

We all need the proper tools in life. Goggles gave me perspective: the ability to see things more clearly and navigate the swimming pool. My goal is that *Feel Better* will provide the tools to give us a better perspective and navigate through life. Just like goggles, understanding my emotional health was something I didn't realize I needed. Just as it's easier to swim with a clear view, it's easier to navigate life with the tools we are going to talk about in this book.

I decided to write this book after a difficult time in my own life and a revelation about the way our society looks at health. I spent a decade of postgraduate education learning about health: four years studying exercise physiology and another six years becoming a doctor. It was no wonder by the time I finished that I really thought I was an "expert" in health; little did I know, I was just an expert in disease.

To me, health meant moving my body daily, eating well, and trying to get enough sleep. That's where the story stopped. Maybe on some level, health also meant not getting one of the horrible diseases I had spent hours studying and learning about en route to becoming a doctor.

It wasn't until the birth of my first son that everything became just too much. Years of running from failure and towards perfection, coupled with a hidden mental health condition, groomed the perfect pathway toward postpartum depression, anxiety, and OCD. A mental health crisis had been brewing for years, but I had no goggles to see it coming.

One day as I was struggling to address my mental health, I sat on my kitchen floor wondering, "How did I get here?" I knew I was missing something: a foundation; I just didn't know what it was. Almost a decade later and I feel like I can now see clearly what I needed.

As a physician who specializes in mental health, I have seen a pattern in many of my patients: distress, hopelessness, and apathy. After speaking with thousands of patients, I realized I wasn't alone in how I felt. Similar to my own story, I found myself offering two things: medications and counseling. Both of these elements are vital and have a critical role; however, I kept asking myself what I could do differently for myself and my patients.

It wasn't until my counselor showed me a list of common thinking traps frequently identified in cognitive behavioral therapy that a light switch turned on. My growing interest in understanding and acknowledging emotions mushroomed into the realization that our emotional wellbeing is the foundation of our overall health. And the fundamental tool that this book seeks to provide—our emotional swim goggles—is self-awareness.

Self-awareness is the ability to understand and monitor your internal landscape and take a good look around. Mental health is built on emotional wellbeing, and the bedrock of emotional wellbeing is self-awareness. Taking another step back, physical health can only be embraced in a healthy way when we take care of our emotional wellbeing and mental health first.

Self-awareness permits meaningful emotional literacy, which means being able to recognize, interpret and acknowledge your emotions. Instead of seeing emotions as annoying and cumbersome, could we see them as clues telling us about what we want, what we value, and what we want to move toward?

Although our emotions come and go, the cascade of our most-common thoughts and subsequent behaviors is where we default to. Like ruts formed from years of use in a road, your brain craves the familiarity of how you are used to thinking and how you are used to behaving–whether this serves you or not. Being aware of these patterns of thought is also important to building emotional literacy.

Too often we let life's emotional bumps in the road affect us without ever taking a step back and asking ourselves the question: "What does this say about my emotional patterns? What does this say about me?" in a curious instead of critical way.

Feel Better starts at the intersection between your emotional and mental health. Let's dive in.

CHAPTER 1

EMOTIONAL
SAFETY GEAR

WE ALL NEED TOOLS

One of my dreams growing up was to be a competitive fig-ure skater. I would look at the athletes training on the ice, spinning and jumping and making it look like they were on any other surface but ice, with its slippery and unpredictable nature. Although my skating career ended before it even truly started, I couldn't wait to teach my kids how to skate. It was a skating instructor that told me on the first day of my four-year-old son's lesson, "The only thing we are going to do today is practice fall-ing." It certainly didn't sound that exciting but we went with it.

Slowly but surely the instructor taught my son how to fall properly on the ice, stating that the only guarantee as a new skater was that he was inevitably going to be practicing these falls many times.

It was such an interesting concept, and one I've held on to for many years. What if it was okay in our life to fall—dare I say to fail? What if it was actually not just okay but encouraged to lose our balance and expected that we would need to find the courage to get back up? What if "practice falls"—or "practice fails" as I like to call them—were just normal parts of life?

WHAT IF "PRACTICE FALLS"–OR "PRACTICE FAILS" AS I LIKE TO CALL THEM–WERE JUST NORMAL PARTS OF LIFE?

Why start a book about mental health with such a story? Because we all experience metaphorical trips and tumbles in life—from losing a job, to major illness, to losing a loved one. That's why it's important to put on emotional health protective gear—and to do it ahead of the fall.

And yet, few of us take the time to prepare for these inevitable slips, even though we can develop our ability to do so. In the chapters that follow, I'm going to introduce you to a powerful process for developing the ability to protect yourself. You'll learn how to utilize proper perspectives to spot emotional clues and what they are trying to teach you about yourself—all to shield you from negative emotional reactions that could otherwise undermine your quality of life and impact your mental health.

Eminent psychologist Dr. Daniel Goleman explains that our mental health is influenced by our emotions as well as our ability to understand and process them. Yet, Goleman notes, "People's emotions are rarely put into words."[1] My job in this book is to help you articulate your emotional reactions in order to better understand and manage them.

And that starts with a little preparation—like putting on a helmet before you slip and fall.

SUSAN'S CHALLENGE

Let me give you an example. For more than a decade, I've practiced family medicine with an emphasis on mental health care. I've seen the impact that working to change our cognitive patterns can have on people young and old. One patient, I'll call Susan, was looking for ways to mitigate the emotional freefall she was feeling and to ensure she was better prepared the next time such feelings invaded her mind.

Susan was a 38-year-old working mother, feeling the pressure of raising a family while balancing other demanding aspects of her professional and personal life. The pressure began to feel like too much. Instead of making time to go for walks or go to her local fitness class, exercise started to drop out of her daily life. Eating on the go became more of the norm, as did working until late at night. All of these fractures of her regular life didn't seem like much in isolation, but in combination led to the reason she eventually saw me: insomnia. After countless nights of poor sleep and trying multiple over-the-counter agents, Susan knew she needed help.

This is not an uncommon story. After sharing her experience with me, the analogy I gave Susan was of a piece of artwork on a computer. The picture displayed is a representation of how we feel overall, and it's what I, as a physician, see. It is often at the root of a patient's complaint, as it was in Susan's case. The pixels that make up the picture are the patient's emotional health, comprising thousands if not hundreds of thousands of emotional reactions that represent our interaction with the world.

Susan began sharing with me a common emotion she had been dealing a lot with: self-doubt. Like many in such a demanding position of juggling work and home, her mind had been plunging into a spiral of self-defeating thoughts. She was ensnared in the mental sand traps of "I should be," "I can't," or "I always." And when she tried to steer her thoughts away from those mental sand traps, something would happen that would confirm all of these beliefs. Whether it was turning in a work project past its deadline or forgetting to buy a gift for a friend's birthday party, the negative thoughts about her worth and abilities seemed impossible to tune out. She felt that regardless of the situation, she was destined for failure. This was taking a big toll on her emotional and physical well-being.

I assured her that she wasn't alone. One of the first steps here is knowing that what you are feeling is not uncommon. Normalizing our feelings is half the battle. I often say anxiety and depression breed in the shadows and fester in silence. Many people who come to me describe a lack of confidence and associated negative self-talk.

I suggested that Susan use the power of anticipation to regain some of her lost self-confidence. All this means is I asked her to start consciously preparing to encounter these negative thoughts and the emotions they would bring up—before they happened. The funny thing about the power of anticipation is that if you anticipate feeling overwhelmed, or anxious, or even flustered, when it actually happens it somehow doesn't feel as strong or scary.

I asked her to try to notice when uncomfortable emotions started brewing under the surface, then to identify *how* those emotions would lead to negative self-talk. I explained that she had likely, without realizing it, been telling herself a story that reinforced the uncomfortable emotions. I told her the brain needs to make sense of the world around it, and sometimes the easiest way to do this is to create a story. In Susan's case her internal

THE FUNNY THING ABOUT
THE POWER OF ANTICIPATION
IS THAT IF YOU ANTICIPATE
FEELING OVERWHELMED, OR
ANXIOUS, OR EVEN FLUSTERED,
WHEN IT ACTUALLY HAPPENS
IT SOMEHOW DOESN'T FEEL
AS STRONG OR SCARY.

story was one of feeling worthless or insecure. A comment by her boss that she could improve on her leadership skills threw her into ruminating for hours about how she wasn't a valued member of the team. This was her way of trying to make sense of her feelings, which were rooted in the story she was telling herself. I explained that the emotions she was feeling were probably based on this negative story, and that she hadn't just told herself, but sold herself on this narrative.

I was hopeful that Susan could become aware of this cycle of triggering uncomfortable emotion to negative self-talk for herself, because once we recognize where and when we have a tendency to tell ourselves something negative (i.e., the trigger) then we can start changing the story to something new. This can be extremely effective in creating new associations between whatever is upsetting us and why we're upset about it. If we can accept that the narrative we are telling ourselves doesn't serve us well (something like, "I mess everything up"), we can then start to think of an alternative narrative, and even with time, try to replace it with something that we believe and that serves us (i.e., "I'm upset I messed up, and I know it's part of learning") The first step of this is acknowledging the story in our heads.

Sounds easy, right? But actually doing it can be a real challenge. Emotions frequently trump logic. Not only are emotions and logic processed in separate areas of the brain; the center relating to emotions is much more closely linked to that of memory and our stories are often born from the way we have interpreted our memories.

EMOTIONS FREQUENTLY TRUMP LOGIC.

For example, to someone who says, "I mess everything up," it may *feel* true even though reality would suggest otherwise. There must be a lot in that person's life that they *do* get right, every day and every week. But getting the emotional self to understand and accept that—well, that's another story. This is where the help of a trusted partner, friend or professional can be extremely useful as we all need help pointing out our blind spots.

Susan accepted my advice. She approached this challenge with vigor. After a few more visits, she told me she was beginning to feel a little more like she was at the steering wheel instead of getting swept away by her emotions. Anticipating the emotion, recognizing the story in her head, and trying to distill fact from feeling were just some of the tools she applied. Instead of constantly worrying about situations, she approached each stressful event like a detective would: with curiosity instead of criticism. She asked, "What are the facts and what are my emotions? Do the two really match up, or are my emotions amplifying a negative narrative I've sold myself?" She said that situations that would have previously led to serious emotional health crises were more bearable because of this awareness. She put on emotional "safety gear" before she encountered uncomfortable emotions.

The goal of safety gear isn't the same thing as bubble wrap; it's not designed to protect you from every bump that comes along—and would you even want that in the first place? The analogy of safety gear illustrates that we all need tools, techniques, and training at various stages of life. Some you acquire along the way; some you are taught, and some you simply have to learn the hard way. In "Feel Better," you will find some tools that will be helpful and others that you might save for later use. The goal is not to change your life immediately but to insulate your emotional health from the bumps and bruises along the way. Of course, each person is unique and may need multiple types of safety gear to handle a fall. But with enough practice, using the methods in this book, anyone can bounce back faster and, more importantly, begin to avoid mental health slips in the first place.

TRAIN YOUR BRAIN

Many people struggle to recognize the narratives they use to explain and justify their emotional reactions. The approach I suggest in this book is based on years of practical application with patients in my practice, as well as some of the best theories on emotional resilience from leading academics and thinkers, including psychologist Daniel Goleman's work on emotional intelligence.

My point is that you are *not* your feelings, thoughts or emotions; you *are* your perceptions. If you want to live a happier life, you have to accept that you are responsible for your perceptions. That's a simple concept, but not an easy one to grasp.

YOU ARE NOT YOUR FEELINGS, THOUGHTS OR EMOTIONS; YOU ARE YOUR PERCEPTIONS. IF YOU WANT TO LIVE A HAPPIER LIFE, YOU HAVE TO ACCEPT THAT YOU ARE RESPONSIBLE FOR YOUR PERCEPTIONS.

Another young woman, let's call her Elizabeth, came to see me because she was feeling anxious before taking tests in school. She didn't want to feel that way. Who does? I explained that it was normal to feel some anxiety before big life events. The question was: How much was this anxiety interfering with her day-to-day life? I explained that we will all have times we don't want to get out of bed, when we feel anxious, or when we get down. I asked her about frequency—was this happening to her more than more than once a month? Every other day? Was it affecting her life a lot?

No, Elizabeth said, it wasn't. But she also said that in all her years of growing up, no one had told her that it was normal to feel anxiety now and then. Her perception was that *any* anxiety was bad, so her emotional health was troubled any time she felt anxious.

Too much anxiety *can* be overwhelming, I explained, but a little now and then isn't going to hurt us. In fact, it can help us focus. It shows we care about what we are doing and how well we are doing it. I explained that she could work on the way she perceived her anxiety, and that would impact her emotional health.

LIKE RUSH HOUR

Consider this: If you commute to work or have ever experienced rush-hour traffic, you have likely experienced an event during your drive that frustrated you. You didn't choose the emotions you felt at that time. Chances are, you didn't say, "Well, that vehicle just cut me off. I think I should be upset, and I select frustration as the right emotion for this situation." No. You just were frustrated. You may have called the emotion "frustration" or "anger" after it came to you, but you didn't *choose* to feel it.

Now imagine that a person who has never driven in a car in rush-hour traffic suddenly gets put behind the wheel. If they get cut off, they might not know what to feel. There's a good chance they'd feel emotions like confusion, fear, and anger. They might lean into one of those emotions, creating a pathway for the brain to react the same way in similar situations. It's hard to make a new connection in the brain. But once a connection is made—say to anger—it becomes easier to follow that path again, even though it leads to something uncomfortable or negative. Remember, your brain doesn't necessarily care whether something is helpful or harmful to you at the moment, what it craves is familiarity.

If you lean into any emotion over and over, it becomes much easier to feel it again the next time something similar happens.

If you're cut off frequently during your commute, becoming frustrated or angry might start to feel like a totally normal part of your day. It can become a habit, and after a while, you might even notice that you are feeling that emotion in additional situations, like when someone on the road doesn't merge at the first opportunity, or when your loved one makes a mistake at home, or when a colleague doesn't say "Hi" in the morning.

We get used to emotions that we feel frequently, even the painful ones. It's easier for us to feel an emotion when we have decided it's justified. And it's much easier for us to feel it again when we've already felt it many times before. Remember, your brain doesn't necessarily care whether something is helpful or harmful to you; what it craves is familiarity.

EMOTIONAL BEDS

Getting comfortable with emotions is like making a bed, fluffed up with feelings we are used to. We tend to return to places where we feel comfortable, and who doesn't love their bed?

Yet while we may impulsively retreat to our emotional beds, thinking they will be safe and cozy, they are usually not comforting at all. Pulling the emotional covers over your head invariably leads you to behave in ways that can cause problems. For instance, it's not good for your physical or mental health to retreat to a self-critical bed like Susan, or an angry bed when in traffic, or a bed made up of any number of painful emotions. We can retreat to many types of emotional beds, yet few are as supportive and comfortable as we imagine they will be.

All this may sound like I am saying that our emotional reactions are completely out of our control. But I have found that while reactions aren't directly controlled by the conscious mind, we *can* use our conscious minds to acknowledge and understand why we react the way we do in certain situations.

This is how we *feel better*.

Beneath our conscious experience is a whole world of dynamic subconscious thoughts and emotions. According to Dr. Shian-Ling Keng and research colleagues from Duke University, being mindful of our cognitive processes can have a powerful effect. In a 2011 report, Dr. Keng explained that simply being aware of our emotions has been empirically shown to impact psychological well-being.[2]

In other words, by cultivating cognitive awareness skills, we can be more competent in our self-care and our social interactions. We can move from simple awareness of what's going on in our minds to gaining an ability to use the strategies I've developed in my clinical practice—tools that can help individuals rise to the challenges that life throws their way. They can become more resilient in their thinking. Rather than letting their thoughts and emotions drag them down, they can use these tools to literally and figuratively; take a step back

That's what I aim to accomplish: To open eyes to the vital links between perception, emotional reactions, and mental health.

To go back to the traffic analogy: Our emotional health is how we tend to react when we are cut off—are we angry or calm, irate or logical? Our perceptions are the way we justify our reactions. And our mental health is not only how we feel overall, but how adaptable we are with our perceptions, because emotional health and perceptions are directly tied to mental health.

That means we need to be more adaptable in evaluating our emotions. This will help us get out of the negative emotions we lean into. Think of it as being an emotion ninja—able to react quickly and effectively to any challenge. And you don't get to be a ninja without some training! You *have* to work at it. In all my years as a physician, no one has ever said to me, "Doc, I don't need to exercise. I just naturally look toned and fit" or, "I don't need to watch what I eat. I maintain a perfect weight and energy-level no matter what I put into my body." Just as we recognize the work we must put into our physical bodies, we must do the same for our mental health. But how?

We have to train our brains.

WHY FEELING BETTER IS PERSONAL TO ME

Two things inspired me to develop the process introduced in this book:

1. Working with patients
2. Working through my own struggle to overcome the power that a negative emotional pattern had over me.

Eventually I learned that we can interrupt negative cycles even when they are deeply ingrained. We do this by developing our cognitive awareness of our emotional reactions, and then taking steps to better manage those reactions.

But that was a hard road for me to travel.

I remember a cold, rainy day in January 2016. I was sitting in the office of a reproductive psychiatrist with my husband and young son. I was a year into motherhood and had been having panic attacks nightly. During the day, I felt nothing but dread. I had difficulty interacting with others.

Anticipating the visit, I had drawn an intricate, color-coded flowchart of all of my symptoms. The psychiatrist looked at my husband and asked, "Is she always like this?"

He nodded yes.

I had been a physician for several years. Ironically, however, I didn't even know reproductive psychiatry existed as a subspecialty. The journey to the initial consultation with this doctor had been a long one. What was supposed to be the best time in our lives after the birth of our first son—a time when people told us to "enjoy every minute"—had felt like a raging whirlpool of fear, despair and shame. I floundered in a constant state of **"SHOULDS"**:

- **"I SHOULD BE ENJOYING THIS."**
- **"I SHOULD KNOW WHAT TO DO."**
- **"I SHOULDN'T BE FEELING THIS WAY."**

I didn't seem to have the right motherly instincts. I felt defective.

Looking back now, I see that in truth the journey to the psychiatrist's office was more like 25 years in the making. I had been lying to myself for a long time and finally the jig was up. My symptoms had started as early as age four or five, when I would develop horrible obsessive thoughts. These thoughts were often about harm coming to a loved one. As I grew older, these thoughts at times could become overwhelming, creating emotions of fear, distress, and panic.

Life continued, but the scary thoughts lurked in the shadows. They remained nameless until one day during a medical school lecture. The professor showed a slide outlining the types of anxiety. Generalized anxiety disorder, panic disorder and obsessive-compulsive disorder (OCD) topped this list. And there, under OCD, was a small asterisk with the words: "Pure OCD: only obsessional thoughts, no compulsions." I immediately went online to research this diagnosis. I could feel my heartbeat in my throat as I read more. Like Tetris blocks, the diagnostic pieces stacked up perfectly. They were describing me.

So I did what every good medical student does when faced with something they need to do to improve their own health: I ignored it and continued with my studies. I felt like just having the words to explain what was happening was enough. I couldn't have been more wrong.

Little did I know that OCD, especially the type with more obsessive thoughts and no compulsions, tends to be more commonly found in postpartum periods. For those who have a pre-existing history, the incidence is much higher.

New mothers can experience various forms of obsessive thoughts, from simply worrying about being a bad mother, to concern that the baby will stop breathing, to fearing that you'll harm your own child. With postpartum OCD, the most challenging thoughts I experienced were those of hurting my child. These are called ego dystonic thoughts—impulses that are repugnant, unacceptable, or inconsistent with one's self-concept. No one wants to have these thoughts, but mothers can become enveloped in fear because of them. It takes great courage to speak the truth, but it needs to be spoken, because too many parents—too many mothers especially—suffer in silence and shame.

So now, here I was at the reproductive psychiatrist's office, with my son in a carrier and my husband beside me. It felt as if I was learning to talk all over again as I struggled to explain my symptoms. Later, I realized that it was less important to explain the symptoms and much more important to simply recognize them. Every second of the psychiatrist asking me questions, looking at me, evaluating me, I was asking myself: "Does she get it? Does this person know at all what I'm talking about? Does she understand me?"

Finally, she leaned in and said, "This is common. This is treatable. There is hope."

It was a moment of clarity. Someone understood! I exhaled. I felt a huge sense of relief, not just as a mother or a woman, but as that little girl who had been so confused and scared all those years.

I had felt anxiety and depression when the perceptions of how family life should make me feel hadn't matched up to my reality. My perceptions, clashing with my emotions, made me feel I wasn't doing enough: that I was a bad mother. And because my reality didn't match up with what I expected, I had been retreating to my emotional bed, a bed full of negative emotions of self-blame, supporting the idea that it was my fault when I didn't feel the way I expected to feel. Now I realized that the only way to change these habits was to disrupt the negative cycle I was stuck in. That day, I knew I had to start working to change the way I thought about my feelings.

As a disclaimer, I continued finding professional help and my clinical diagnosis was integral to understanding my cognitive and behavioral patterns as well as uncovering the lessons I will share throughout this book. I highly encourage anyone who feels like they are struggling to seek mental health care with a professional counselor, psychiatrist, or doctor.

THE SIX STEPS

I present to you here the six steps I've used for years now to help people overcome emotional challenges from chronic anxiety and depression to a lack of self-worth. Each step is designed to help restructure both conscious and subconscious thinking, and to improve quality of life by improving emotional, mental and physical health.

The following chapters are devoted to each of these steps. For now, here's a quick overview.

1. **Prepare.** Lay the foundation by understanding the stress equation.
2. **Acknowledge.** Learn to recognize what I call "sticky" emotions and thoughts that come into your mind. Realize that these thoughts or emotions do not have to be permanent, and that they do not define you.
3. **Awareness.** Acknowledge your emotions as they are. Replace the labels "bad" and "good" with "uncomfortable" and "comfortable." Remember that emotions are clues, not truths.
4. **Accept.** Choose to act on an emotion or to let it go. Don't put effort into emotions that don't serve you.
5. **Act.** Understand the emotions you are feeling. Then decide whether or not to act. In this way, you can reframe the emotions that affect you the most.
6. **Talk.** Communicate with others about the emotions you feel. Seek help from empathetic people who will understand. By doing this, you can remove any stigma that surrounds what you are feeling.

I've seen people young and old use these steps to revise their normal routines and thought patterns. The results have been inspiring to me. The Six Steps help people who feel trapped in negative emotional cycles to break those patterns and feel better. That's the reason I have such a passion for sharing these tools.

In the coming chapters, you'll discover what leads you to fall into the false comfort of your emotional bed. You'll find yourself thinking more deeply about your reactions to everyday situations. And, most important of all, I hope you will learn to train your brain to think in new ways. Then you'll be able to control your reaction to emotions that can come along without warning and sweep you away.

Before all of that, though, I need to tell you two truths and a lie. Let's go to Chapter 2.

CHAPTER 2

THE SCIENCE
OF EMOTIONS

LEARN TO MAKE SENSE OF WHAT'S GOING ON IN YOUR HEAD.

Most of us think about our bodies fairly often. If we have a sore muscle or a headache, we search for a way to ease the pain. We are very aware of and worry about gaining weight; it might affect our health or appearance. Each day we look in the mirror to make sure we are presentable, we comb our hair, we check our makeup.

But when it comes to our emotions, how much do we understand their influence on our bodies as well as on our behaviors? Emotions are underappreciated by most people. Yet much of what occurs in our everyday lives is driven by emotions: We pursue what we think will be rewarding; we strive to avoid what we think will make us unhappy.

TWO TRUTHS AND A LIE

One of the best places to start is to dispel the myths many of us grew up with surrounding emotions: things we believe yet aren't true.

Take the list below: Are these true or false? What were you taught as a child? What do you believe now as an adult?

1. **Emotions are either good or bad.**
2. **You are your emotions.**
3. **Your brain's job is to keep you happy.**

The short answer is that all three statements above are false. It might seem obvious on a conscious level now, but think back to your childhood; what did you observe? For most of us, learning about our emotions was done implicitly, not explicitly. We watched the ways our parents reacted when they got frustrated; we might have paid a price when we showed our own "big" emotions and we quickly learned that there were certain things we felt and other things we simply didn't.

1. EMOTIONS ARE GOOD OR BAD

Next time you see a painting that catches your eye, take a look at the colors in it. Is it just yellows and pinks and light blues or are there darker, more intense colors like maroon, olive, and charcoal gray?

What you quickly notice is that darker, richer colors give paintings the depth we so admire. Emotions are no different. Many of us grew up thinking that we weren't allowed to feel those "darker" emotions like anger, resentfulness, envy, or jealousy; as if feeling these "bad" emotions meant that somehow it translated into our identity as a person. There is no such thing as a good or bad emotion: Emotions are simply comfortable or uncomfortable. Remember too, just because an emotion might be "uncomfortable," that doesn't mean we don't gravitate towards it if it is familiar (remember: the emotional bed).

> **THERE IS NO SUCH THING AS A GOOD OR BAD EMOTION: EMOTIONS ARE SIMPLY COMFORTABLE OR UNCOMFORTABLE.**

2. YOU ARE YOUR EMOTIONS

Alice, a 17 year old, came into the office one day as a new patient. I didn't know much about her and was looking forward to learning more during our time together. As I entered the room I could tell this might be more of a challenging encounter. Her eyes didn't shift up from the floor; her response to all of my questions was a shrug or one-word answer, and her body language seemed to scream "When will this appointment be over?" The only thing I had to work with were depression and anxiety assessment tools that she had filled out prior to the appointment. I could see by her scores that she was struggling with her mental health.

I did something I usually don't do: I started filling the silence by talking. I told her that other patients I had seen with scores like she had would tell me they felt like their mood was low, like they didn't have the energy to do the things they loved, and even if they did, they didn't seem to get as much pleasure out of them. I then told her some of these patients would even tell me they felt guilty or worthless at times; it was at this point she looked up at me and for the first time in the entire appointment made eye contact. It was like I had finally struck a nerve. I'll never forget the words she said. She looked at me and with an expression that was hard to read, she simply said "I **am** worthless."

Emotions are "energy in motion"; they come and they go. The only pitfall is that many of us start to wear our emotions like an oversized parka: it becomes a shield against the world, something to identify with and base future decisions on. Take Alice for example; she might have "felt" worthless at one time but by repeating this over and over again, her "I feel" had translated into an "I am," integrating into her sense of identity. Unfortunately as I found out later, it wasn't just Alice telling this to her but some of the family members she lived with as well, therefore just reinforcing this negative self-deprecating dialogue.

MANY OF US START TO WEAR OUR EMOTIONS LIKE AN OVERSIZED PARKA: IT BECOMES A SHIELD AGAINST THE WORLD, SOMETHING TO IDENTIFY WITH AND BASE FUTURE DECISIONS ON.

One of the simplest ways you can notice this is the next time you feel an emotion, ask if you are telling yourself "I am angry" or that "I feel angry." Notice the difference here. One is telling your brain that you are an angry person, and done enough times, you even start to believe this and use it as justification for future behaviors. The other highlights the effervescent quality of emotions, such that they come and they go. Telling yourself "I feel" instead of "I am" gives you full access to the palette of emotional colors without feeling that it is suddenly a part of your personality.

TELLING YOURSELF "I FEEL"
INSTEAD OF "I AM" GIVES YOU
FULL ACCESS TO THE PALETTE OF
EMOTIONAL COLORS WITHOUT
FEELING THAT IT IS SUDDENLY A
PART OF YOUR PERSONALITY.

3. YOUR BRAIN'S JOB IS TO KEEP YOU HAPPY

There are many times I endeavor to build rapport with my patients, and if that takes talking about current celebrity events, movies or video games, I'm more than happy to partake. On one particular occasion, one of my patients, Julia, was gushing over her favorite celebrity makeup tricks she had seen on social media the other day. After listening to her "ohh" and "ahh" over how gorgeous she felt her favorite stars looked, I asked her, "What do you admire about yourself?" The question caught her a bit off guard but she immediately replied to me, "I love my left eyebrow." Now it was my chance to feel a bit taken aback by her answer and I couldn't help but ask, "What about your right eyebrow?" to which she vehemently replied, "Are you kidding me?" It turned out to be a great opportunity to talk about the role of the brain in keeping us happy. I told her that the brain is really good at doing three things:

- **Comparison**
- **Critiquing**
- **Cautioning**

We never get to hear what is in other people's heads so it can be helpful to hear what comparison, critiquing and cautioning actually sound like. Below are some examples:

Comparison in our head sounds like:	"See, they always," or "See, they never."
Critiquing in our head can sound like:	"I always," or "I never," or "I knew I couldn't."
Cautioning in our head can sound like:	"Don't," or "Watch out for," or "You should be."

We tend to be much more adept at telling ourselves what we DON'T have rather than what we DO have. From an evolutionary perspective this negativity bias makes complete sense. You needed to know when you didn't have enough food or water, if your shelter couldn't withstand the elements, or if you were too far from your tribe. All this attention to what you needed or what you didn't have was protective; however, in the age of abundance and instant gratification, this translates into wanting what you deem you don't have. Social media only fuels this fire by increasing comparison, such that now you can see and know everything about an acquaintance's incredible holiday before you even get out of bed in the morning.

Somewhere between the waddling toddler and the adolescent growth spurt, a child's inner voice turns from one of curiosity and wonder to self-criticism. Playing a game of baseball in the park, my husband gently pitched to a five-year-old girl playing for the first time. When she swung and missed, she immediately said, "See, I told you girls cannot play baseball." Without even knowing the words, she had so eloquently illustrated confirmation bias. Notice how it is much easier to enter the self-critical mode "I can't," "I don't know," or "I always" versus trying to troubleshoot. Curiosity might come to us innately as a child, but to foster it requires two key prerequisites: self-compassion and self-acknowledgement (more on this in later chapters.)

CURIOSITY MIGHT COME TO US INNATELY AS A CHILD, BUT TO FOSTER IT REQUIRES TWO KEY PREREQUISITES: SELF-COMPASSION AND SELF-ACKNOWLEDGEMENT.

WHAT ARE EMOTIONS?

Before I dive further into the science, it's important to take a minute and define the terms: moods, emotions, and feelings.

"A mood is described by the American Psychological Association (APA) as "any short-lived emotional state, usually of low intensity." Moods differ from emotions because they lack stimuli and have no clear starting point. For example, insults can trigger the emotion of anger while an angry mood may arise without apparent cause.[3]

Emotions are often confused with feelings, but the two are distinct. Emotions are how we respond to an event or situation, and more specifically, the stimulus of this event or situation. Imagine you just found out you are pregnant. Your first reaction to this stimulus (in this case the positive pregnancy test) might be one of joy and jubilation. Unconsciously, you might also be fearful or apprehensive at this huge milestone and change it might bring in your life. There can often be a mix of emotions present for any stimulus, something I often call an "emotional sandwich": layers of various emotions all in response to the same stimulus.

Your emotional reaction also brings into context your background: your upbringing, your lived experiences and perhaps your ethnic and cultural lens.

Emotions are made up of three components: They begin with *subjective experiences*, also called a stimulus or a trigger. These might be anything from seeing a favorite color to losing a loved one. They are subjective because the experience will evoke unique feelings in each person. For instance, one might feel anger at the loss of a loved one while another may experience sadness. Next, emotions create **physiological responses**. These are the result of the autonomic nervous system reacting to the emotion in physical ways. Finally come **behavioral responses**, the actual expression of the emotion that is important in showing others how we are

30

feeling. Behavioral responses might include a laugh or a sigh—or other reactions depending on societal norms and the personality of the person experiencing the emotion.

This perception of sensation is what we call "feelings"; in this way, feelings can be a component of emotions. In the example above, the woman who just found out she is expecting might feel her chest bursting with happiness or a sensation of feeling queasy as she realizes the all too familiar morning sickness. Feelings can also arise from changes in our homeostasis such as feeling tired, hungry or cold where there isn't an overlying dominant emotion.

WHAT'S IN THE STIMULUS?

It's important to understand that we can best prepare to control our reactions to life events by learning to be curious about our own emotions. And that starts with understanding triggers.

Canada Life's Workplace Strategies for Mental Health puts it this way: Triggers are automatic responses to specific stimuli. Triggers can be people, places or things, as well as smells, words, or colors. Emotional triggers can also be automatic responses to the way others express emotions, like anger or sadness.

For example, you may not have a problem interacting with an angry person but find it hard to deal with someone who's crying. The opposite may be true for others. Emotional triggers stir up very specific emotional responses in us. If we react with extreme discomfort when someone cries, then crying is an emotional trigger.[4] Triggers are connected to specific stimuli, experiences, and memories. The brain connects previous interactions with similar emotional triggers to the current situation at hand. We might not even be aware we are doing it.

Let's say you were bullied in third grade by a fellow student who liked to wear a yellow t-shirt. Today, 30 years removed from that childhood trauma, you walk down the street and feel a surge of fear. You might not even be aware that you passed a stranger in a yellow shirt. Heck, you might not even remember the bullying from childhood. But the stimulus is bringing up memories and thoughts of that past experience. The feeling is very real, even if you don't exactly know why it's happening to you.

Without some serious introspection, we're more likely to blame the situation if we don't understand *why* we react the way we do. For example, on the busy street, we may think to ourselves, "I don't like crowds."

Here's how we process emotions:

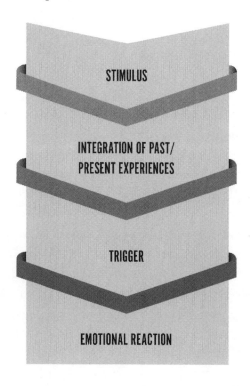

- Before emotions arise, there's usually a stimulus.
- Our memories and past experiences influence our interpretation of the stimulus.
- When we have similar emotional reactions to certain stimuli—like someone crying or angry or even someone wearing a yellow shirt—those stimuli may be triggers for our emotions.
- When we identify the stimuli that trigger our emotional reactions, we can start to work toward calming our reactions and choosing more helpful responses.

When we understand what we are feeling, we can step back and question what triggered it.

SEEING EMOTIONS AS "KEYS"

We have all seen that comedy sketch on TV where someone goes to open a door and pulls out a key ring with about 100 keys on it. Maybe there is someone locked on the other side waiting to get out and now the audience moans in desperation as they anticipate how long it will take to try every single key.

What if we thought of emotions as keys? Some keys open the door and need further exploring into a new environment with curiosity. Some keys help close the door to things that potentially no longer serve you. Notice here I'm not saying escape, ignore, suppress or deny. It is an active process of accepting you have the key (i.e., the emotion) and then deciding whether you want to approach or avoid where the door leads.

Another great analogy is that of a compass. Psychiatric counselor, Madhuleena Roy Chowdhury, says, "Much like a compass that guides us in the right direction, emotions have the power to guide us to the right actions." She cites the example of how fear might keep a child from confessing a mistake; however, parents most likely will discover what the child did anyway. So in this case, listening to fear is futile. On the other hand, for someone who encounters a bear in the wild, fear that motivates them to avoid confrontation may lead to a life-saving decision.

> "MUCH LIKE A COMPASS THAT GUIDES US IN THE RIGHT DIRECTION, EMOTIONS HAVE THE POWER TO GUIDE US TO THE RIGHT ACTIONS."
>
> —MADHULEENA ROY CHOWDHURY

"It is crucial to judge when to trust emotional triggers and act on them and when not to," she explains. "It is essential for us to understand how to regulate or control our emotions so we [can] use them optimally. Self-regulation is all about pausing between feeling and reactions. It encourages us to slow down for a bit and act after objectively evaluating a situation."[5]

Unlike how the old trick of "Don't think of a purple polka-dotted elephant" works (okay, what did you JUST think of?!), telling yourself you "feel fine" doesn't usually work.

Parker says that the best way to prepare to deal with difficult emotions is to develop mindfulness.[6] It's easy to envision mindfulness as a type of exercise you need to be doing while adopting a lotus posture, but this is far from the truth. Think of mindfulness as simply creating space between you and your emotions. Imagine yourself sitting at the end of a lake watching the ripples form: the ripples come and go; these are your emotions; you are simply the observer.

Another important way to prepare is to work on emotional regulation. Clinical psychologist Nick Wignall offers some tips on the emotional regulation skills we should each develop:

1. *Hit the pause button.* "Once you've paused, ask yourself: *What's going on here?* When we can inhibit our instinctive response to negative feelings and approach it with an attitude of curiosity, our chances of managing the situation intelligently go way up." Consider your automatic thoughts, which are our default, initial interpretations of what happens to us.

2. *Self-awareness.* Identify the feeling or feelings; try to give them a name.

3. *Identify the trigger.* "Once you've used a sudden, strong emotion as a cue to pause, the next step is to identify what event triggered your response in the first place."

4. *Generate alternative thoughts.* "Come up with more interpretations than your first automatic one. This practice creates mental flexibility, a key component in the ability to disengage from negative thinking patterns and overwhelming emotion. "For example, you might replace thoughts such as 'My boss hates me' or 'I am no longer needed here' with alternatives such as, 'My boss is upset at this moment,' or 'I know I am hard-working and honest, let me give it another try.'"

5. *Re-rate the intensity of your emotional response.* "After generating multiple (hopefully more realistic) alternative thoughts, return to your emotion(s) you identified in Step 2 and reassess their intensity. Almost always, they will have gone down at least modestly as a function of questioning your automatic thoughts and generating alternative and more realistic ones."

6. *Self-compassion and emotional support.* Set aside some time for yourself each day. Remind yourself of your talents and virtues. Seek support within yourself by practicing mindful

self-awareness—or outside yourself through communication with others.[7]

EMOTIONS AND OUR VALUE SYSTEM

We think long and hard about many of the events that impact us and the emotions that arise. The problem is, most of us don't think about our perceptions very much at all. Therein lies the tool I'm providing. We can't change emotions that happen to us, but we can look back and consider how we perceive each event.

The way we perceive the world is deeply tied to the way we think the world *should* work. The values we have developed and hold dear—like fairness, equality, or compassion—have tremendous influence over our emotions.

The brain usually goes through a very quick three-step process each time we experience something that elicits emotion.

1. We tap into the <u>values</u> we have developed and hold dear.
2. Those values influence the way we <u>perceive</u> the event that is impacting us.
3. We have emotional <u>reactions</u> to those events based on the way our reality lines up with our values.

The thing is, as much of this happens unconsciously, most of us aren't even aware we have gone through this process in the first place.

In the coming chapters you will learn that emotions leave three clues; one of the most important is significance, i.e., helping to shine a spotlight on what you value.

Remember the example I used in Chapter One, about how our perceptions can influence our emotional reactions when we are driving in rush-hour traffic? Let's say you really value fairness; it might really bother you when someone cuts in front of you. If you stop at your initial reaction of anger and frustration, you will be missing this important piece of information and discovering that fairness is a really important value system of yours. Of course none of this is to justify or condone bad behavior but it does allow us to create some space between our initial reaction and our perception of the situation.

COMPLEX AND BASIC EMOTIONS

Paul Ekman, a prominent American psychologist, identified six basic emotions that can be recognized by facial expressions: happiness, sadness, fear, anger, surprise, and disgust.[8] Then in the 1980s, psychologist Robert Plutchik countered that research by identifying eight basic emotions, grouped in pairs as opposites:

- Joy/Sadness
- Anger/Fear
- Trust/Disgust
- Surprise/Anticipation

Plutchik concluded that these emotions trigger behaviors with high survival values, such as the way fear inspires the fight-or-flight response and makes the heart beat faster .In addition to basic emotions, Plutchik argued that humans can experience 34,000 unique emotions, termed *complex emotions*. Some are a combination of other emotions. (For example, it's possible to have more than one emotion going on at the same time, or to experience conflicting emotions simultaneously, such as love and hate for the same thing or the same person).[9]

Further research at the University of California, Berkely concluded that humans have 27 types of emotion, all of them interconnected, and "richer and more nuanced than previously thought."[10]

My interpretation is that we can boil this down to four basic emotions that we all can relate to:

- **FEAR**
- **HAPPINESS**
- **ANGER**
- **SADNESS**

In other parts of the world, grief, for instance, looks different. Resentment, mourning, or guilt is expressed differently among cultures. But those four core emotions are maps to the human face and body. If I see little kids in the Philippines shrinking away, eyes wide, mouth open, wrapping their arms around themselves, I know they're in fear. If the corners of their lips are turned up, cheeks raised, muscles around the eyes tightening, they're probably happy. That's why these four emotions are called basic. They are also called basic because when you filter down all the other complex emotions, you can usually put them into one of these buckets—fear, anger, happiness, or sadness.

FUNNEL OF FEAR

Most of us have a funnel somewhere in our kitchen: that nebulous kitchen tool we hardly use but when we need it, seems irreplaceable. For those who have toddlers at home, perhaps you have used one to pour sand through.

There's something satisfying about the process of going through a metaphorical funnel: of taking something bigger and complex and distilling it down into something more simple and easy to digest.

Think of an emotion like feeling worried, worthless or betrayed; if you were to distill it down into all of its parts, there often is a common denominator: fear.

Fear isn't something we talk a lot about in our society; in fact we start at an early age to reinforce that we "shouldn't" feel scared or that we need to "be brave." It's not something that we know how to talk about freely. When was the last time you asked your partner or close friend, "What are you afraid of?" Besides spiders, heights and public speaking, we don't tend to talk about our fears in great detail.

Let's say you participate in a staff meeting and no one seems receptive to the new customer service plan you have carefully laid out. You walk out of the meeting feeling an emotional sandwich: fatigued, depleted, rejected, perhaps envious of a colleague who got a better response—or even fearful of the fate of your job. Most of us are overwhelmed even with this influx of emotions, so we do what we have been trained to do: we try to suppress it. We distract ourselves on our phones, we have a sugary caffeinated drink, or we promise ourselves an extra glass of wine at home.

My theory is that at the foundation of many complex emotions, especially uncomfortable complex emotions (i.e., the emotional sandwich described above) is fear. If you were to take a pestle and mortar and grind complex emotions into fine grains of sand, these would be fear. The hard part is, talking about our fears is something we simply aren't used to doing.

The good part is that once we identify the same root fears, they often show up in our lives in many ways. In jest, I love to say that "every day is Halloween to our fears"—they just adorn different

IF YOU WERE TO TAKE A PESTLE AND MORTAR AND GRIND COMPLEX EMOTIONS INTO FINE GRAINS OF SAND, MANY OF THESE WOULD BE FEAR.

costumes masquerading as "different problems," when in reality, at its core it is the same fear. Take a look at the list below and see if you can relate to any. If so, how do they show up at home, at work, or in your relationships?

Some examples of common deep fears I often see in my practice:

- Fear of Failure or Inadequacy
- Fear of Uncertainty or Lack of Control
- Fear of Not Being Good Enough
- Fear of Being Alone, Abandonment, Isolation
- Fear of Rejection
- Fear of Loss of Freedom
- Fear of Something Bad Happening
- Fear of Judgement

The problem is that uncovering our fears can be difficult; it is unfortunately a lot easier to just address life's issues as they arise like a makeshift "whack a mole" rather than unearthing the core issue.

Try this exercise:

EXERCISE: 7 LAYERS DEEP

Think back to a time when you were dealing with a complex and possibly uncomfortable emotion, perhaps envy, resentment, disappointment, or frustration.

Really think back to the situation and try to put yourself back in this time period.

The seven-layers-deep exercise is a metaphor for digging deep into the earth—with every shovel you are getting deeper to the "core" of what you are actually feeling. The way that you get beyond a complex uncomfortable emotion is by asking yourself, "What would that say about me?"

Use this as an example: A patient's mother complained to our front desk about a prescription I had written for her daughter.

My immediate response: frustration, disappointment

Q. Seven-Layers-Deep Exercise: Ask yourself five-to-seven times, "What does it say about me that the patient's mother called in to complain about me?"

A. The staff would think poorly of me.

Q. What would it mean if the staff were to think poorly of me?

A. They would think that I wasn't competent as a physician.

Q. What would people say knowing that the staff think that I am not competent as a physician?

A. They might not trust other clinical decision I make, or they may think less of me as a physician

You keep doing this over and over again, and eventually you might unearth your underlying fear.

In this case, my underlying fear was "fear of failure" or "fear of not being good enough."

Often we need help with this, whether it be the help of a trained health care professional like a counselor, or even just a trusted, close friend.

EMOTIONAL INTELLIGENCE

For the most part, emotions are constructive. They are influenced by what is good for us, what we learned during our upbringing, and what we believe will be best for society as a whole. Our emotions guide our behavior in a way that should lead us to positive outcomes. However, emotions can become destructive if they are no longer the appropriate response for a situation, or if subconscious emotions cause reactions that we are unable to understand. Being in touch with your emotions is called "emotional awareness." Being able to be emotionally aware with ourselves or with others and turning your understanding into action is referred to as "emotional intelligence."

The term "emotional intelligence" was first coined in 1990 by social psychologist Peter Salovey, who later became the president of Yale University, as well as psychologist John D. Mayer of the University of New Hampshire. It was popularized in the 1995 book *Emotional Intelligence: Why It Can Matter More Than IQ*, written by psychologist and science journalist Dan Goleman. Salovey, Mayer, and Goleman define emotional intelligence as the ability to recognize, understand, and manage our own emotions as well as recognize, understand and influence the emotions of others.[11]

Emotional intelligence (EI) has now become a science of its own, with practitioners around the world. While some psychologists argue that we are either born with EI or without it, research shows that emotional intelligence can be improved over time.

Those who develop their EI can use their understanding of their own emotions and the emotions of others to move toward personal and social growth. Those with low levels of EI may not understand what's going on inside their minds. They may find it hard to control their emotions. They also have little hope of understanding the emotions of those around them. This can leave them feeling powerless, frustrated, and unable to express what they are going through, as well as unable to empathize with significant people in their lives.

Take 19-year-old Eli for example; he told me how growing up he was often "baby sat" in drug houses. It wasn't uncommon for him as a five-year-old to see adults passed out on the ground due to intoxication. He described one particular incident where he saw a close friend almost die of a drug overdose. I couldn't help but inquire how he was coping now over 10 years later. He told me that he had learned to forgive; that he certainly had anger, resentment, shame and disappointment for the childhood or lack thereof but realized, in his words, "I didn't want the cycle to continue." Eli allowed himself to feel the necessary emotions and process them over the years. Having a high EI doesn't mean you simply numb yourself of emotions; it is actually the opposite. If you're at a stage where you have both acknowledged and accepted your emotions for what they are and consciously move forward on your own terms you have a high degree of EI.

Salovey, in an article co-authored with other Yale faculty members, presents a four-branch model for emotional intelligence. He identified four skills:

1. *Perception of Emotion.* "Perception of emotion refers to people's capacity to identify emotions in themselves and others using facial expressions, tone of voice, and body language ... Those skilled in the perception of emotion are able to express emotion accordingly and communicate emotional needs."

2. *Use of Emotion to Facilitate Thinking.* "People who are skilled in this area understand that some emotional states are more optimal for targeted outcomes than others." In other words, if emotions are clues, these people are good at picking up the mystery.

3. *Understanding of Emotion.* "EI includes the ability to differentiate between emotional states, as well as their specific causes and trajectories. People skilled in this area are aware of this emotional trajectory and have a strong sense of how multiple emotions can work together to produce another."

4. *Management of Emotion.* "Emotion management includes the ability to remain open to a wide range of emotions, recognize the value of feeling certain emotions in specific situations, and understand which short- and long-term strategies are most efficient for emotion regulation."

Goleman, who popularized the study of emotional intelligence, also introduced the idea of an emotional quotient (EQ) score similar to IQ as a measurement of someone's emotional intelligence aptitude. Goleman argued that EQ counts twice as much as IQ and technical skills combined when it comes to becoming successful.[12] He's not alone; other researchers also argue that it plays a bigger role. *New York Times* best-selling author Chade-Meng Tan says that high emotional intelligence is linked with better work performance, makes people better leaders, and creates the conditions for personal happiness. "If you are able to perceive an emotion the moment it is arising, that gives you the power to turn it off if you want to. It gives you choice," Tan says. While turning off emotions is not like the flip of a light switch, it is something we can get better at. "And that's life changing," added Tan. Emotional awareness leads to self-assessment, and that allows you to "get to know yourself a bit better... This is what I'm good at, this is what I'm bad at' ... 'This is what I really like to do, this is what makes me happy,' and so on.[13]

THE INVISIBLE CHALKBOARD

I like to have people visualize it this way: Each day we walk around with an invisible chalkboard floating above our heads. The chalkboard includes the story we are telling ourselves in real time as well as our past experiences that shape and color this story. Do you ever notice people at the airport or the mall—coming and going, weaving through the lines and wearing an expression that suggests they are a million miles away? It's not just that they have somewhere to go or some place to be, it's that they have a story that influences the way they see the world.

Let me give you an example. I was recently on an airplane ready to embark on a five-hour journey across the country. I sat beside a lovely couple who had recently returned from what sounded like a luxurious cruise in the tropics. It would have been easy enough to leave the story there at which point I would have created the impression of two very relaxed and now tanned people who loved enjoying themselves and had the time and resources to do so. I would have been so wrong. We got chatting further and I soon found out what was written on her invisible chalkboard. She had become pregnant at the age of 15 and had gone back to complete her studies at the age of 30 including her master's degree. She had been raised by a single mother and experienced an adult's share of responsibility at an early age. She had lost a loved one to cancer last year and it was because of this that she and her now-husband had seized the opportunity to start living their life. All of that was on her invisible chalkboard.

Sometimes we wonder, "Why did they react that way?" or "What led them to make that decision?" Judgment usually follows; it is usually the easiest path. If we only knew that person's invisible chalkboard, our thinking could be guided by empathy and compassion rather than segregation. I see this all the time in my patients. It's easy to judge the 17-year-old who ended up in the ICU with pancreatitis from drinking too much alcohol. If only we could be privy to their story; if only we could hear about the years of neglect, of witnessing abuse and of trying to find their own way in an entirely unpredictable environment.

Remember, the invisible chalkboard isn't an excuse to act a certain way to or make decisions that put yourself or others at risk. What it is, however, is an explanation, simply an explanation, an insight into the WHY.

Try this exercise:

EXERCISE: INVISIBLE CHALKBOARD

Think about the following categories. Note that these are just suggestions; there are many more.

- Family
- Work
- Finances
- Health
- Relationships
- Hobbies and Interests
- Loss

Then ask yourself these questions:

- What are some things even my good friends might not know?
- What have I been too afraid to share or acknowledge about any of these categories?

Next, grab a journal and pen. Without fear and shame, begin to write freely … category by category. How are you doing? What is going well? What is not going well? What are you worried about? What is weighing you down? What do you wish could be different?

Lastly, consider sharing your list and your thoughts with someone you trust. Being vulnerable can be hard, but it is actually an avenue of connection. By opening up to others, you realize that people are more alike than they are different. Those who open up are viewed as more likable and trusted. This psychological phenomenon is known as the "beautiful mess effect",[14] and I—personally and professionally—have found it is aptly named and indeed beautiful.

In an effort to be vulnerable, let me share some of my categories and concerns.

Health: Suffered with a mental health diagnosis since the age of 4–5 (pure OCD), lived in shame and secrecy until my late 20's where I finally discovered what I was experiencing

Work: Often struggle with a fear of failure or fear of 'missing something' as a physician

Family: Often feel incredibly overwhelmed in my parenting journey. Juggling work, speaking, writing and motherhood can make me feel like I have too many browser windows open at all times.

Family: Watching family members struggle with their own physical health has been extremely difficult

THE OPTIMAL HEALTH PYRAMID

Let's face it, most of us are focused on the center of the pyramid when we think about our overall health (mental and physical). We're well aware that to be healthy we need to eat healthy, get rest, and exercise. Of course, for many people this is easier said than done. When your life gets busy, sticking to a healthy regime can be hard. And even for those who do make healthy choices, often these changes don't have as significant an impact as they would like. However, I tell my patients that focusing on the body alone is not enough to make meaningful changes in how we feel.

The optimal health pyramid demonstrates the importance of understanding how our social, emotional, and physical health work together.

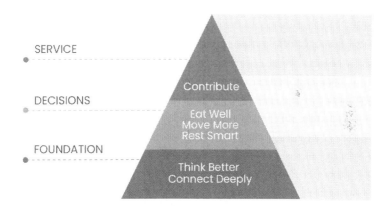

Health is a series of decisions we make every day, not a destination. It is standing in the Starbucks line and figuring out whether you actually need the extra shots of syrup and whipped cream. It's deciding to stand up from your desk and go for a 10-minute walk during your lunch break. It's saying "no" to that next episode that inevitably appears within 10 seconds of watching your favorite Netflix show. These decisions are cumulative and together they do make an important difference.

When my postpartum OCD and depression were at their peak, I really felt like I could "yoga" my way out of the state I was in. I remember getting so anxious and worked up as the yoga video loaded as if to say "I can't wait another second to relax right now." Not to say that exercise, sleep and nutrition aren't important—they are critically important, hence the reason they are included; however, the concept I completely failed to ignore was everything I am about to teach you in "Feel Better"—how I could train my brain.

Take a look at the bottom of the pyramid - the foundation. At the base we see two key aspects - train your brain and connect deeply. These were two fundamental pieces I was missing in my personal journey. I had isolated myself and stopped investing in my close friendship. In addition, I failed to recognize that to train your brain you must not only be aware of your emotions, thoughts and feelings but your perception of the situation.

Your perceptions are inextricably linked to how you make decisions about your health (the middle of the pyramid). Without healthy perceptions, even the most well intentioned diet and nutrition program can be detrimental. For example, someone who is overly worried about healthy eating may not get sufficient nutrients with an overly strict diet. Or someone who is overly concerned with working out might continue to exercise when injured because of an unhealthy perception of gaining weight if they miss a day. Contrast that with those who have a healthy perception of wanting better health and quality of life; they would allow for rest and flexibility in their diet now and then.

Embedded within the Optimal Health Pyramid are what I call "emotional highlighters." Imagine taking a chunky vibrant yellow highlighter and highlighting a paragraph in a textbook. What does this do? It puts a spotlight on the text and draws your attention to it. Similarly, sleep—or lack thereof—stress and nutrition (namely hunger) are all emotional highlighters. They enhance and put a spotlight on the emotion you already have. We all know that feeling of being hungry, tired, or stressed and sometimes all three; think back to a time like this. Whatever emotion you were feeling suddenly feels amplified, perhaps even too much to deal with it. In cases like this, where you feel like the emotions are too big, go back to other aspects of the pyramid and ask yourself, "Do I need to eat something nutritious?" "Do I need to rest or take a nap?" "Do I need to move my body?"

SLEEP—OR LACK THEREOF—STRESS AND NUTRITION (NAMELY HUNGER) ARE ALL EMOTIONAL HIGHLIGHTERS. THEY ENHANCE AND PUT A SPOTLIGHT ON THE EMOTION YOU ALREADY HAVE.

Next, at the top of the pyramid, we find the concept that is now well established: if you truly want to be happy, go out and help someone else. Our ability to see ourselves as not just an "I" but a "we"—as part of something bigger than ourselves and contributing to something greater than us all—has a profound impact on our mental health. In one study that has now been replicated many times, participants were given either $5 or $20 and asked to spend the money on themselves or others. Several hours later, participants were asked to rate their happiness levels. Those that spent money on others (i.e., prosocial spending) were significantly happier, independent of the amount of money they received in the first place.

Each part of the pyramid builds on and interacts with the other parts. This holistic view of our health allows us to achieve a balance and harmony that helps us feel better about ourselves, our interactions with others, and our ability to do good in the world. But, it's important to note that optimal health begins with building healthy perceptions and recognizing how they influence our emotions.

MAKING SENSE OF IT ALL

If we find ourselves feeling stressed, annoyed, or deflated, it's important to take some time to understand why. When we develop the ability to identify our emotions and understand their causes, we are in a much better place to address what is going on inside us with appropriate responses and action.

Over the next chapters, I'm going to introduce you to the six steps to help you improve your emotional awareness, take control of your emotions, and be better prepared when the winds of change hit us— as they inevitably do. The six steps help people to stop focusing solely on eating well, sleeping well, and exercising regularly, to focus on our perceptions and our minds in a deeper way and contribute within a supportive community.

This process will help you start to recognize your emotional triggers, build on your strengths, and understand that your values and goals are affecting your thoughts and behaviors. The benefits are better relationships, lower stress levels, the diffusing of internal and external conflict, and improvement in achieving overall life satisfaction.

Let's get started.

CHAPTER 3

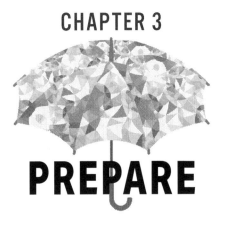

PREPARE

DEVELOPING YOUR EMOTIONAL SAFETY GEAR

B enke Blomkvist is the coach of Swedish Athletics for sprint hurdles. Over his career, he has trained and mentored a world-record holder, a European champion, and top finishers at the World Championships. He says, "We had a [video] picture on the wall, and I stopped the video in positions, and we discussed, 'Okay, can we hit these positions?' and apply the principles of good hurdling."[15] By showing techniques used by the world's most successful runners, Blomkvist helps his athletes improve. And then, of course, there comes practice, practice, practice.

That's not dissimilar to developing good techniques for dealing with emotions, thoughts, and feelings. We can study how others succeed, envision ourselves doing the same, and then practice. As we do this, we are developing our own emotional safety gear.

In life, we all face hurdles. Sometimes many come in a single day. But there are some simple techniques that can help us prepare to conquer them in the right way, with the right technique. We can recognize that:

- *Hurdles will come.* No one is immune from challenges.
- *Facing hurdles might make us feel uncomfortable.* Having feelings that are undesirable does not automatically mean we are doing anything wrong.
- *Recognizing and responding to your* emotions takes practice. It is not an on/off switch. Some days are better than others. Your only job is to foster a sense of curiosity and know that this is something we ALL need to practice.

This chapter explains how we can develop emotional safety gear by preparing for uncomfortable feelings. It will also teach how to reduce the impact such feelings may have on your mental well-being.

THE GOLD NECKLACE

My parents came to Canada as refugees. Thrown out of Uganda by dictator Idi Amin in 1972, they were lucky to arrive here to begin a new and safer life. I would listen to my parents recount the stories of their traumatic upheaval with as much awe and apprehension as I could muster as a young child. I remember hearing about this dictator who had a dream that all people with "brown skin" should leave the country. I remember how my mother, the eldest of 4 children, told me how they had less than 72 hours to pack up all of their belongings and consolidate their life into a single suitcase. She told me stories of how she used to jump across the equator line, and how she would enjoy the warm tropical climate of East Africa, only to come to Vancouver, British Columbia which made up for its rainy climate with the warmth of the people that welcomed them.

These stories—loss of home, loss of community, loss of belongings —are, unfortunately, not uncommon. Despite hearing the pain and sadness in their voices as they recounted arriving in Canada with little to nothing and having to rebuild, their voices were also brushed with hope and even gratitude. My grandmother always told me, "Canada has been very good to us". She was an avid volunteer until her 80's and always believed in giving back to her community; something that she promised herself she would do the moment her feet touched Canadian soil. As she grew older and her knees started aching and her body began to feel like it was fighting against her, I would often ask her "Mama, how are you feeling?" to which she would simply reply "I am very well, my complaints department is closed." She used to tell me that each one of her children were like pearls; I wish I had told her more often that she was like the gold necklace that held these pearls in place: sturdy, unwavering, and full of sparkle regardless of the external circumstances.

My grandmother's perception of the situation—of being forcefully removed from her country, of having to start again from scratch with a young family and of having to navigate her sense of identity in a new cultural context—could have been very different. She could have been resentful or full of hatred and contempt for what had happened to her. The irony of the situation is that it is often through suffering that we find a sense of meaning. Sometimes we come to this conclusion quickly, other times it can take years, even decades.

What stands in the way is often our obsession with trying to control things that are out of our control (i.e., managing our expectations) as well as looking at the situation in only one way (i.e., our perceptions).

REMEMBER THIS FORMULA

I once gave a keynote presentation to a group of accountants, who gravitate toward logical thinking and formulas. I spontaneously wrote this on the whiteboard:

Your Desired Outcome = Great Expectations x Perceptions

Having suffered from a form of OCD for most of my life, I knew early on that I wasn't just the sum of my thoughts or my feelings—some of which could feel overpowering at times. There was something else that made me who I was. I realized the missing piece was my perceptions.

Let's break down each part of this formula, starting with Great Expectations:

GREAT EXPECTATIONS

When we wake up in the morning, most of us have expectations for the day. We may even feel that we are already either ahead or behind in what we hope to accomplish over the next 14 or so hours before we head to bed again. Maybe you woke up early, exercised, showered, ate a healthy breakfast, and feel that you've already exceeded what you expected to do by that time of day. Or, if you're like many of us, perhaps something happened to throw you off your game. Maybe you slept through the alarm. Maybe you spent too much time on social media or your news feed in the morning. Maybe your kids missed the school bus and you

YOUR DESIRED OUTCOME = GREAT EXPECTATIONS X PERCEPTIONS

had to hand each of them a Pop Tart as you scrambled into the car to get them to class on time. Few of us ever get to noon saying, "I am exactly where I need to be right now,"

Of course, expectations are important. They allow us to complete our schooling, hold down jobs, and be good parents. The problem comes when we assume that we can always meet our expectations through things we *can* control, like due diligence and best effort. A lot of our expectations can be thwarted by things that are completely out of our control.

As psychotherapist Amy Morin says, "There's a brutal truth about life that some people refuse to accept—you have no control over many of the things that happen to you."[16] But you do have the ability to adjust your expectations.

For example, I remember something that happened to me in seventh grade that shows what can happen when expectations and reality collide. It was the last week of school; our teacher passed out yearbooks. Most of the students raced to get theirs signed and to sign for friends. As usual, I lingered in the background. I was an introvert, unknown and shy.

The activity of racing around to get signatures didn't attract me. I found comfort in academics, and that did little to enhance my social life. Yet I longed for someone to sign my yearbook.

Suddenly a fellow student approached me. He was not just any student; he was a boy I'd had a crush on for two years, although I had never said more than "hello" to him. His sudden presence unnerved me. Before I could say anything, he grabbed my yearbook and signed it. My first entry, and it was from *him!* I felt my heart beating in my chest. I wondered what secret feelings he might reveal.

He tossed the book back at me and rushed off to autograph others. I tentatively opened the page he had signed. There, in large scratchy handwriting, was his message: "I hope you can tutor me in high school."

The adult in me loves this story because it illustrates the concept of differing expectations. I had expected a secret declaration of love, while in reality he just wanted help with math. The point: We have expectations for most situations in our lives, but rarely do expectations match reality. If we let these mismatches control our emotional reality, we are in for a disappointing life.

FOCUSING ON THE HOW, NOT THE WHAT

We live in a *What*-obsessed society. *What* is your grade, degree, or product? We give such things a lot of accolades. *How*, on the other hand, rarely receives the attention it deserves.

Think about an undergraduate student who becomes president of her student union, volunteers to help with various campus organizations, competes in a chess club, and consistently earns top grades. At first glance she might seem to have it all together. But what if you found out she suffered from often crippling anxiety, headaches caused by chronic lack of sleep, poor eating habits, and, at times, isolation from her friends? You would quickly realize that *what* she is doing differs greatly from *how* she is doing.

Here's a personal example. My family and I recently went hiking. We took a trail that was a bit too difficult for my three-year-old son. At the halfway mark, my two older sons proclaimed adamantly that they expected to make it to the top. But the three-year-old was exhausted and couldn't continue. My husband and I could tell that we were in a difficult situation. If we went down, my younger son would be happy, but my two older boys were bursting with unspent energy and would feel like they hadn't finished the hike. If we went up, my husband or I would have to carry our youngest.

So we adjusted our expectations. My husband explained to my two older sons that the hike today wasn't about getting to the top. Instead, it was about doing something new and adventurous, exploring the wilderness, sharing time as a family, and getting some sunshine. By reframing our expectations, the older boys' obsession with getting to the top started to give way to expecting a pleasant time together as a family. We wandered back down the trail, spotting birds, examining moss on trees, and considering our family outing a win. Even though we might not have achieved the "what" (i.e., getting to the top), shifting our attention to the "how" brought us back to the moment at hand.

Think of it this way: Acknowledge the "what" and focus on the "how." Of course you need to acknowledge WHAT happened and the accompanying emotion (disappointment, frustration, anger). However, the second, and often-forgotten step, is shifting attention to all of the factors that are in your control, the most important of which is how you showed up.

> **THINK OF IT THIS WAY: ACKNOWLEDGE THE "WHAT" AND FOCUS ON THE "HOW."**

Notice here changing our expectation had nothing to do with effort. The effort, focus, and determination you fuel a task with is completely up to you. It is the realization that even DESPITE this, things might not always work out the way that you've planned. It is this clarity, this freedom in many senses that becomes your superpower. Often, we are so concerned with performance, outcomes, and productivity that we refuse to accept what is beyond our control. Is it possible to be achievement-focused and yet know when some things just cannot be changed? Absolutely.

As our family learned, the way individuals interpret and react to events *can* be controlled, at least to some extent. Amy Morin continues: "Sometimes, all you can control is your effort and your attitude. When you put your energy into the things you can control, you'll be much more effective."[17]

Stanford University Professor Dr. Carol S. Dweck's work on a growth mindset describes the shift from outcome (the what) to effort (the how). As parents, we might be fairly adept at using this concept, but when it comes to incorporating it into our own lives, it may feel foreign. Focusing on effort vs outcomes is more than simply throwing compliments at yourself. It requires strategy. First, you must understand the intention behind the exercise. If you truly want to *feel better*, you must learn how to "think better" and thinking better requires rehearsal and repetition.[18]

Try this exercise:

EXERCISE: FOCUS ON EFFORT

1. *Think of a recent situation that fell below your expectations.* (Mine: I recently went to Walmart with my boys and one of them had a massive tantrum in front of the whole store)
2. *Recognize what your expectations were and why this experience fell below your expectations.*
3. *Recognize that part of the situation was beyond your control.*
4. *Acknowledge that you feel upset, stressed, or overwhelmed by what happened.*

5. *Shift your attention to* how *you reacted.* (Mine: I wanted to scream but was able to remain calm, even though it was difficult.)
6. *Notice what went well and celebrate that.*
7. Ask yourself what you could improve on.

To appropriately deal with expectations, we must become much more curious about how the brain processes events such as these. We must evaluate not only what we expected to happen, but also what caused that expectation and why we feel the way we do about the result. When results don't match expectation, most of us default to self-criticism, because that's what we're familiar with (the "emotional bed" I introduced in Chapter 1). But to foster curiosity you must dive into a deeper pool of inner acknowledgement (more to come in Chapter 5).

As a leader (and that includes parents, coaches, and so on), one of the most powerful things you can do is to notice the *how* before the *what.* I recommend adopting the ratio of five to one. Comment five times about the *how* for every one comment about the *what.* For example, if you are a manager, comment on *how* your employees perform, show up, interact with customers, and offer ideas in meetings, and do it five times as often as you talk about what the result was. Due to the negativity bias explained previously, our brains are really good at focusing on the things that are going wrong. Imagine a spotlight on a stage, shifting to illuminate various actors and scenes. Imagine being the camera operator and shifting this spotlight constantly to pick up, i.e., "notice," all of the things that are going well right before your

COMMENT FIVE TIMES ABOUT THE *HOW* FOR EVERY ONE COMMENT ABOUT THE *WHAT*

eyes. I sometimes do this with the adolescents I work with. They might tell me "My life sucks" or "Nothing is going right today." I encourage them to do the "spotlight" exercise and try to notice five things that are going right. It could even be as simple as waking up in the morning, eating breakfast, showering, coming to class, handing in an assignment, and drinking water.

For parents, I recommend the same ratio. It is normal and natural for children's bad behavior to get your attention, because sometimes the bad can be dangerous, troublesome, or just down-right uncomfortable. But if you put a spotlight on all of the things that are happening but often go unnoticed: sharing a toy with a sibling, asking for something instead of grabbing, putting their shoes away—you'll find that both effort and output will improve.

THE POWER OF PERCEPTION

Remember the formula Great Expectations x perceptions. Let's focus on perceptions now.

We are not our thoughts; we are not our emotions. Perhaps, just perhaps, we are our perceptions. A perception is how we choose to see the world; it is the story we tell ourselves. When we are able to examine our perception and see it for what it truly is and could be, this is true self-awareness. The people we surround ourselves with, our previous experiences, and our upbringing all play a crucial role in influencing our perceptions.

> **WE ARE NOT OUR THOUGHTS; WE ARE NOT OUR EMOTIONS. PERHAPS, JUST PERHAPS, WE ARE OUR PERCEPTIONS.**

Think of perception as a kaleidoscope. As a young child I used to love to play with those hand-held kaleidoscopes. Every turn of your hand the image would change from a rainbow to a mosaic to a flower. This is exactly how our perception works. One slight shift and we can make ourselves see a situation in a completely new way. If the image in the kaleidoscope is our change in perception, the looking glass is being self-aware enough to recognize this. Self-awareness allows us to appreciate why we feel the way we feel and why we do what we do. It helps us recognize the stories we tell ourselves to explain why the world around us seems the way it does.

Remember, however, that it is difficult to gain perspective if you are too attached to certain perceptions. Understanding your emotions requires you to have a certain capacity to examine yourself, to stand back from your emotions and observe them objectively. It is a matter of being curious, not critical.

John was raised in a home where any effort, however small, was recognized and praised by his parents. His wife Cynthia, however, was raised in a home where meager effort was often greeted with sarcasm, seen by her parents as a challenge to improve performance. Shortly after they were married, John cleaned the kitchen, did the dishes, and took out the trash. He expected to hear something from his wife like, "Thank you. Nicely done." When Cynthia said nothing, he pointed out to her what he'd just done. Cynthia replied, "That's what I do every day. What do you expect, a gold star?"

"How we perceive others and situations has everything to do with how we were raised, experiences we have had, how we have been taught values and morals, and examples in our lives," says Certified Diversity Practitioner Suzanne Combs-Brown. "Those all go into how we form perceptions of others and their actions. That's exactly why your perception, my perception, and their perception, can all be different."[19]

Combs-Brown adds, "Our perceptions influence how we focus on, process, remember, interpret, understand, synthesize, decide about, and act on reality. The problem is that the lens through which we perceive is often warped by our genetic predispositions, past experiences, prior knowledge, emotions, preconceived notions, self-interest, and cognitive distortions."

To overcome all of that, Combs-Brown suggests we need to continue to discover our blind spots.[20] That means we need to ask more questions and look for authentic connections with other people to share the good and bad in our lives—people who might be able to open our eyes. Through these steps, you can move from acknowledging your emotions and perceptions to preparing to do something about them. You can move beyond an immediate emotional reaction to a more logical action based on knowledge and understanding of yourself. And the more we understand ourselves, the more empathy and compassion we develop. This helps us feel better about ourselves and helps us understand and feel better about others, too.

Closely related to self-awareness is something I term "inner acknowledgement." This is not the same as self-love; it is a recognition of three things: 1) Your own personal progress (recognizing how far you have come and in doing so the potential you have for change), 2) Purpose (changing your view point to "I-focused" to "other-focused") and 3) The place you have in the world (otherwise known as "mattering," or the impact you have on others). Inner acknowledgement doesn't have to be rooted in achievements. It is the unique ability to see that you have merit, you are capable of improvement, and you can have a positive influence on those around you. More to come on this in Chapter 5.

INNER ACKNOWLEDGEMENT DOESN'T HAVE TO BE ROOTED IN ACHIEVEMENTS. IT IS THE UNIQUE ABILITY TO SEE THAT YOU HAVE MERIT, YOU ARE CAPABLE OF IMPROVEMENT, AND YOU CAN HAVE A POSITIVE INFLUENCE ON THOSE AROUND YOU.

THE GLUE BETWEEN EXPECTATIONS
AND PERCEPTIONS: VALUES

I met a young man once who had come to see me for low back pain. I was working in an office within a school and many of the youth who attended this school had been in difficult life circumstances. When asking this young man about his family history he succinctly told me that he didn't know anything about his mother or father. His mother was in and out of rehab and his dad was in prison. The look on my face must have conveyed something because when he met my eyes he simply said "Don't feel sorry for me; I see myself as a person with potential." It happened years ago but it's a moment I have never been able to forget. We went on to talk about his goals and dreams. He wanted to become a mechanical engineer as he loved math. He acknowledged that his past had been tough but he also appreciated his mom for getting the help she needed. He knew a path to a better life would be through education and he knew he wanted to focus on this. It was clear to me that he valued self direction, the capacity for improvement, and a sense of freedom. This is not to say he didn't struggle or wish for a different upbringing. This example, however, illustrates so well how our perception and expectations are shaped so much by our values and what we believe to be true.

> **DON'T FEEL SORRY FOR ME; I SEE MYSELF AS A PERSON WITH POTENTIAL.**

Here's a personal example. I have three young boys. Each one has various things that they value. One of my sons is highly attuned to what he feels is unequal or unfair. Fairness is written in bold letters on his invisible chalkboard. One year on Halloween night, I was dividing a pile of candy that the boys had collected at a community event. I thought there was plenty of chocolate and other treats to go around. Everyone was going to get a nice collection.

Without a lot of thought, I pushed the candy into three piles that were roughly equal. I figured there was no need to count out each piece. But my son, who values fairness, felt intensely that what I had done was unfair. He was quick to point out that I had not carefully counted the candy. He felt it needed to be divided according to type and total number into precisely equal amounts. Resigned to accommodating him, I took the time to split the piles by the type and the exact number of pieces, all under his careful watch. Then, he was content.

Here's the rub; we think long and hard about many of the events that impact us and the emotions that arise. The problem is, most don't think about our perceptions very much at all. Therein lies the tool I'm providing. We can't change our emotions, but we can look back and consider how we perceive each event.

Our perceptions influence the way we align our values with our reality. The way we choose to see an event will help us see if it aligns with our values or not. We might not be able to control our values, but the way we perceive reality can be controlled.

Remember the example I used in Chapter One, about how our perceptions can influence our emotional reactions when we are driving in rush-hour traffic? By managing our perceptions, we can reason with our emotional brains by taking a second look at the story we tell ourselves. That story may please us in the short-term: we may actually enjoy feeling resentful, frustrated, or over-whelmed. But those feelings can be detrimental in the long run. For instance, if we value fairness, someone cutting in line in traffic might upset us because they haven't paid the price of waiting in line like everyone else. However, by changing the story to, "Wow, that person must be late for something important," we can start to influence the way we feel.

Try this exercise:

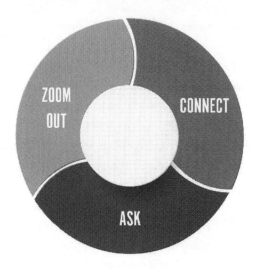

Developing proper perception is both an art and science. I encourage my patients to use a few techniques to help shift their perceptions.

The first is to **Zoom Out**. My eldest son has recently been experimenting with the zoom lens on a camera. He was excited to see how he could bring an object closer and then farther away while remaining still himself. Can we zoom in and out on our emotions? Absolutely. We can become so rooted to what we feel. But you have probably noticed that your attitude toward a situation can change if you allow some time to pass and zoom out.

You've probably benefited by removing yourself from a challenging situation, just by zooming out and giving yourself some space. Ask yourself "Is this permanent or temporary?" or "Will I remember this in 6 weeks, 6 months or 1 year?" Likely the answer is no. The adage "It's now, not forever" helped me immensely when I was dealing with postpartum anxiety. Creating a temporal bracket around events helps you assess things with a more long term perspective.

The next technique is to **Connect**. One of the pillars of self-compassion is to form strong relationships, to connect with a social network of people who will help lift you or at least empathize with what you are going through. Take a moment to think of a recent event that stressed or overwhelmed you. Working with others who have experienced what you are going through, who care, and who you know will support you can help immensely. This not only creates connection by helping you to feel you are not alone, it also fosters compassion toward others who are going through similar situations.

The third technique is **Ask**. Asking yourself the question "What would someone I respect do in this situation" can be incredibly useful to gain some insight into a challenging situation. This person could be a friend, a celebrity or even a religious figure.

Alternatively, coaching yourself through the problem by referring to yourself in the third person (ie. using your own name) compared with using the word "I" can be a simple and effective technique of tapping into the part of your brain that is less reactive and impulsive and more logical and clear sighted.

Try this:

What would (fill in the name of a person your respect) do in this same situation?

Next time you find yourself struggling at home, work or school, talk to yourself using your own name and see how this changes the flavor of the dilemma you face. Does this help you get some mental space?

These three techniques are just a starting point to help us prepare to tackle tough emotions. Another key factor in dealing with both expectation and perception is acceptance. It may seem ironic, but accepting the outcome—good, bad, or otherwise—makes it easier to move on from anything you face. Resistance and rumination breed resentment. Accepting the outcome and your emotional reaction to that outcome may be hard, but acceptance is a vital part of moving on. Accepting that a situation didn't go the way you envisioned doesn't make you lazy or lenient; it simply helps you identify what is, and what is not in your control. Acceptance of your emotional reaction to a situation also allows you to create some space and helps you see that you are more than your emotions and feelings.

HOW TO MAKE THE HURDLES NOT QUITE AS HIGH

We began this chapter with the story of hurdles and circle back to it now as it underscores the fact that we cannot change life's challenges or unpredictability. That is the nature of this world. The hurdles might remain; what we can change is the perceived height of them, making them feel in some sense that they are easier to navigate.

A story I'm not proud to share but is comical nonetheless is ironically related to hurdles. It was a grade-three track meet and I was competing in the hurdles event. I certainly wasn't a confident runner; I definitely didn't enjoy sprinting, and given my adult height today is only five feet one inch, let's just say I wasn't winning any awards in the long jump. Hurdles, on the other hand, were tolerable. We all stood in our sun hats and polyester pinnies waiting for the whistle to blow. Without hesitation I took off sprinting down to face each hurdle head on. I didn't realize I was about to take this in the most literal of senses as I catapulted over my second hurdle, stumbled completely and collapsed to the ground. Now in those milliseconds that followed I could assess the following: I was shocked at what happened, I actually wasn't that hurt, and the only thought that rang as clear as day in my head was "I don't want to finish this race." So let's just say I "prolonged" my injury, I hobbled off to the sideline clearly appearing that my body couldn't finish the race and after that, hurdles soon went under my list of things to avoid at the track meet.

Why am I telling you this story? To make you smile? Perhaps. To demonstrate that unfortunately we can't always clear life's hurdles? Certainly. Most importantly it is to give you a visual picture of the thing we all want to do sometimes: just not get up. Stay down, crawl your way over to safety and don't think about what lies ahead. When you need this "time out," of course take it; just know that when you are ready, your new emotional toolkit will be there to help you with the next challenges.

FEEL BETTER WITH THESE RESOURCES

Take the free Optimal Health Quiz and get a glimpse into y health.

https://drshahana.com/optimal-health-pyramid/

Want more? Follow me on my journey to build emotional clarity and capacity here:

My website is: www.drshahana.com

https://www.youtube.com/@dr.shahana-feelbetter

www.linkedin.com/in/shahana-alibhai-feelbetter

https://www.instagram.com/@thedrshahana

CHAPTER 4

ACKNOWLEDGE

RECOGNIZE EMOTIONS AND THOUGHTS FOR WHAT THEY ARE.

When you go to the doctor, you probably hear questions like: "How is your sleep?" "How is your appetite?" or "Where is your pain?" Those are pretty standard questions. But what if your physician asked you: "Do you care about yourself the way others who love you do?"

Initially I didn't know how to ask the question, but I knew it needed to be addressed. There is this dichotomy between patients showing up to me wanting to feel better, and their intrinsic attitude towards themselves. The answer of one youth in particular cut right to the point; when I asked him "Do you care about yourself?"

DO YOU CARE ABOUT YOURSELF THE WAY OTHERS WHO LOVE YOU DO?

He just looked at me and said "Are you kidding? I f—ing hate myself."

Not everyone's answers are so blunt but there was something that got me thinking a lot about the need to address this question.

I remember one patient; I'll call her Sam. She was 22 years old and had grown up as a twin. From in utero, she had been compared to her sister. Now 22 years later, her sister had graduated from an elite college while Sam pivoted from job to job, moving across the country in the process. In the background of all of this, Sam had been able to end and leave an abusive relationship with a man much older than she was. She was now in a relationship and found herself self-sabotaging things, despite her partner caring deeply about her. She found herself getting jealous if he looked at other women, creating a narrative in her head that justified why "someone like him" would never be with "someone like her."

Our conversation that started initially for anxiety quickly morphed to the central themes of low self-worth, insecurity, and jealousy. Behind the anxiety were the feelings of not being worthy of love. I remember looking at Sam and saying, "No degree could ever teach you the courage and strength it must have taken to leave that abusive relationship." In this simple statement she received something she had been craving for so long: acknowledgement.

You see I thought the answer was always in self-love. Just "love yourself" and then you can do the work, right? No. Not even close.

Prior to that conversation I hadn't spent much time thinking about self-awareness, self-acknowledgement, and self-love. But now I found myself face to face with the need to explain these concepts to my patient. I had always considered self-love to be an overused, nebulous idea. Loving yourself is, of course, important.

But simply telling my patient that she needed to love herself wasn't going to meet her needs. She needed to know how to get there.

The pathway to feeling better begins with acknowledgement, crosses a bridge called awareness, and leads to a place of compassion. So, let's travel that path together. By doing so, we can learn to honestly look at our own feelings and emotions, accept them for what they are, and deal with them in appropriate ways to achieve a positive outcome.

Even in my patient who admitted to hating himself, the truth is that everyone wants to care about themselves enough to feel better, and to feel better enough to care about themselves.

START WITH INNER ACKNOWLEDGEMENT

My dad used to take us skiing growing up. As the youngest, I was fortunate that I would always be paired with my dad on the chair lift while my elder sister would have to yell "single" in the lineup for the hopes of a partner to pair up on the two-person chairlifts. That was until the invention of the three-person chair lift! The moment I'm about to share has been etched in my memory for over 20 years and you will soon see why. It was just a typical day at the ski hill and my sister, dad and I were about to take our place to catch the three-person chair lift. Any skier out there knows the process of glancing behind your shoulder so you see the chair coming, putting your butt back on the seat and lifting your skis in the air to clear the ground, and away you go. Well, that's ideally how these things work. I found myself seated and soon airborne next to my dad, the only issue was that my sister had been knocked to the ground by the lift. I looked back and there she was, being taken care of by the ski staff as they moved her out of harm's way.

THE PATHWAY TO FEELING BETTER
BEGINS WITH ACKNOWLEDGEMENT,
CROSSES A BRIDGE CALLED
AWARENESS, AND LEADS TO
A PLACE OF COMPASSION.

I remember spending the entire chair lift yelling at my dad that we had to "immediately stop the lift" and craning my neck back to see if my sister was ok, which thankfully she was.

The image of me in the air, suspended from cables, with my head cranked behind me is the perfect metaphor for the importance of looking back in time and seeing how far you have come. How often do any of us do this? In the case of Sam, it took me reflecting back at her the tenacity, courage, and perseverance she had to leave a relationship that was both physically abusive and emotionally manipulating.

Let's consider a teenager; I'll call him Braden, who came to talk to me about his mental health. I learned that at a very young age he started experimenting with cannabis, alcohol, and drugs. Now, at 17, he was vaping, smoking cannabis occasionally, and drinking on weekends. But he had given up other illicit substances and wanted to further reduce his consumption of alcohol. "I'm so frustrated that I keep drinking even when I tell myself I want to cut down," he said.

I congratulated him on wanting to cut back and on recognizing that this would improve both his physical and mental health. However, what I did next surprised him. Instead of focusing on his next step, I asked him to take a minute to look at how far he had come. I repeated what he had just told me, that at age 14 he found himself using multiple illicit substances and falling into a dangerous spiral of abuse. Now, just three years later, through his own effort, he was clean of multiple substances with a goal to decrease the use of others. To me this was remarkable.

I asked Braden to complete a simple but powerful exercise. It's called measuring your success backwards. I asked him to do what I had just done, to look at where he had been and compare it with where he was now. You can do the same with anything you've gone through.

Try this exercise:

EXERCISE: SELF ACKNOWLEDGMENT

Draw a horizontal line on a blank sheet of paper or use the space on the next page. On the left mark childhood and on the right, mark your current age (i.e., present day).

1. Above the line, add in experiences you perceive as positive. These could be graduations, marriage, birth of children, or moving into a new house? Note: just because they are perceived as positive doesn't mean they are not stressful.

2. Below the line, critically think over the years where the greatest challenges have arisen and over what time period. Challenging might be unexpected; it might be things that were out of your control, or it might be situations that were difficult to exit. Add these events into the timeline, below the line.

3. Circle two of the challenging experiences and two of the positive experiences. Now consider this:

    How did you show up in those situations? Was there a trait, a habit, a skill that served you? Take my postpartum journey. Although having my first child was a positive experience, the postpartum journey would definitely fall into the challenging timeline. There were many things I wished I had done during that time but if I had to really stop and think about one trait/habit/skill that got me through it would be courage. From picking up the phone and calling the crisis line, to seeing the reproductive psychiatrist, starting medications, sharing my story of postpartum OCD, all of this required an immense amount of courage to overwrite the program seared into my brain: the fear of not being perfect.

This exercise shows you several things.

- You can and have made progress on goals before.
- The person you are now and the person you were, several years ago, are different. This means change is possible.
- You have probably achieved more and come further than you give yourself credit for.

POSITIVE EXPERIENCES

CHILDHOOD ─────────────────── **PRESENT DAY**

CHALLENGING EXPERIENCES

WHAT IS YOUR HOUSE MADE OF?

Most of us can recall the story of the three little pigs; each built their house out of a different material to deter the wrath of the big bad wolf. The pig who built their house out of straw or sticks didn't last long against the wolf's "huff and puff." The pig who chose brick, solid and unyielding—well they faced a much more fairy-tale-worthy happy ending.

There are times when our house, the sense of who we are, our self-concept, so to speak, feels fragile, even threadbare. It feels like it doesn't take much for us to spin out like a ball of soft yarn. There are other times where we feel steadfast in our shoes; we feel grounded in our relationships, we have a sense of purpose in our jobs, and although life isn't easy by any means, we know what we stand for.

There is no right answer here; the question is merely asking "What is your house built out of?"

Maybe the better question is "How do you turn the straw or sticks into bricks?

Remember from Chapter 3, the only thing we are in control of is the HOW, not necessarily the WHAT.

I meet many patients who, if something they perceive adverse happens to them, assume it directly says something about them. If they weren't accepted into their program despite a stellar application, if they were rejected when it came to making the basketball team, or if they weren't invited to a coveted party—all of these things would "say something" about them, their character, their self-worth.

Remember the three "Ps" introduced in Chapter 3: this is how you turn your sticks into bricks.

PROGRESS: Train your brain to recognize all of the 'small wins'. Write them down if you can. Remember, don't measure the 'what' or product but the 'how' you go about it. If your goal is to go for a walk every day after dinner and one day you go for 5 minutes consider this a 'win' because it's not the duration but the habit you are building.

PURPOSE: We tend to think of purpose like finding a buried treasure—as if once you "find it" you will finally understand the reason you exist on this earth. This "all-or-none" way of thinking about purpose can actually make those of us who are struggling with this concept in general think that we are "failing" at yet another thing. What if we started living our life *with* purpose rather than *for* a particular purpose? What if rooted in the definition of purpose was simply to be more "others"-focused and shifting the spotlight from what we need to how we can be a part of helping someone else in need?

PLACE: Identifying that you have a place in this ecosystem. There are people that rely on you just like you rely on and need other people. We all need this sense of "mattering." Although this concept was first studied decades ago, Dr Gordon Flett, author of "Psychology of Mattering," has helped propel this concept to popular media. According to Flett, mattering can be thought of as "feeling like you belong in a group" and being "missed by people in that group if you weren't there." It certainly shares psychological elements with concepts such as self-esteem; however, the research has found that both are distinct.[21] A more succinct definition by Dr Isacc Prilleltensky, professor at the University of Miami and co-author of "How People Matter," is "feeling valued and adding value." The sense of mattering has been coined "double-edged," pertaining to the fact that high levels of mattering can be thought of as protective and fostering resilience while lower levels of mattering are thought of as destructive and increasing one's vulnerability to mental health issues in the future. [22]

A measure to reflect this is called the anti-mattering scale; this is not the same as just lacking a feeling of mattering but rather that individuals who score high on this scale feel they, at some level, might not be worthy of mattering. High scores on the anti-mattering scale have been associated with lower emotional regulation and reduced life satisfaction, as well as higher levels of perceived stress, loneliness, anxiety, depression, and suicidal ideation.[23] As per Flett et al in the paper entitled "How and Why Mattering is the Secret to Student Success: An Analysis of the Views and Practices of Award- Winning Professors," "anti-mattering experiences can leave people feeling invisible, unheard, insignificant, and irrelevant".[24]

To summarize, use past success to plan for future success. This sounds easy, but it can be challenging. For some reason, even when I ask myself to do this exercise, I tend to rebel a little, partly because we find it hard to celebrate our own wins. At a deeper level, we also worry that acknowledging our progress—recognizing how far we have actually come—might give us permission to take it easy, to slow down. We may wonder, "Is self-acknowledgement really just permission for self-leniency?" "Does it make me more self-indulgent?" and "Won't it make me take my foot off the gas rather than going full speed ahead toward my goals?" Evidence answers these questions with a resounding, "No."

This inner acknowledgement is what makes self-awareness accessible and doable. Realize that to begin you don't have to love yourself—or even like yourself. All I ask is that you do the exercise above and realize how far, in one or multiple areas of your life, you have come. Give yourself the permission to notice not only *what* you have achieved but *how* you achieved it. This can contribute to a robust feeling of self-acknowledgement.

Your brain is very malleable, and positive thoughts about yourself create neural connections that are strengthened every time you repeat them, says Vered Kogan, founder and CEO of the Momentum Institute, an organization dedicated to helping leaders develop appropriate skills and mindsets, especially in the face of change. According to Kogan, "The stronger the neural connection, the more it shapes what you believe to be true about what you can or cannot do. Your mindset then influences your thoughts, emotions, behavior and, ultimately, your results."

Kogan adds that by acknowledging and celebrating yourself more often, "you physically alter your brain to notice more evidence of your capabilities and success. You can program yourself to believe that you deserve good things and that you are capable of creating positive changes in your life. As you strengthen those belief systems, you can experience even more confidence, resilience, and motivation."[25] This feeds directly into Beck's Cognitive Model of Depression.[26] When you look back and see your "wins" and how far you've come, your core beliefs about yourself, others, and the world shift in a new and positive direction.

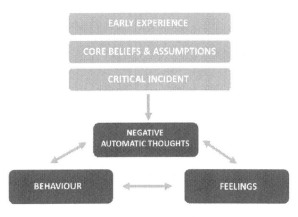

A cognitive model of depression (adapted from Beck, 1976, 1979), The Open University.

Try this exercise:

EXERCISE: THE PAC TABLE

1. **PROGRESS**: Each step you have taken on the way to learning a new skill (no matter how small) especially towards the things you value in your life.

2. **ACKNOWLEDGEMENT**: Acknowledgement you have received from others (let it sink in); these include compliments from others. Receiving gratitude is perhaps one of the most potent forms of gratitude practice. Dig out old birthday or holiday cards and keep them in a more accessible place. Re reading these notes of kindness, appreciation and love can be paramount in helping us acknowledge what others see in us.

3. **CHANCE**: We often judge ourselves based on the outcome of our decision. What if the emphasis was in whether you had the courage to take the opportunity or 'chance' in the first place? Taking a chance means flirting with the unknown and increasing our tolerance for uncertainty is another way we can bolster our self acknowledgment.

SELF-AWARENESS

I'm short: only 5'1 on a good day. I remember growing up needing to even have a step stool to put my clothes on shelves, or to reach things on higher shelves. I think of acknowledgement as a step ladder. Why not take a step for a better chance of success? Countless books and podcasts talk about the power of self-awareness and how to cultivate it. So why aren't more of us doing it? Because it's messy! I compare trying to become more self-aware to using the step ladder to look into that back closet you have thrown things into for 20 years, and now are finally going to start cleaning out. No one wants to do it. It's much easier to keep throwing things in and shutting the door—until one day the door refuses to close!

Self-awareness is the ability to monitor your inner world. It means that we sincerely strive to evaluate what we are feeling. We become curious, in the sense that we want to understand *what* we feel and *why* we feel that way. We see clearly that when we are in a situation where our emotional reactions make us feel uncomfortable, we can step back and understand what we are feeling. We can clarify the emotional patterns that we are predisposed to assume. We can acknowledge fear; we can acknowledge pain; we can even begin to acknowledge the voice of shame. Acknowledging our emotions can help us change our emotional bed.

It can be helpful to think of internal self-awareness and external self-awareness as two separate buckets. Internal self-awareness pertains to understanding your inner landscape and why you feel and even behave the way you do; related but distinct is external self-awareness, which is being able to tune in to cues from others, both verbally and non-verbally, in order to understand how others see you.

With internal self-awareness in particular, the topic of saliency becomes especially important. I'll never forget my first-and-only debut as an actor. It was in an elementary school play titled "The Runaway Snowman." My part, police person #3, had one line exactly "Lost, nowhere to be found." I remember the feeling as my fellow police people and I scoured up and down the isles pretending to look for the "runaway" snowman. When it was time for my line I felt the heat of the spotlight on my back and the rest was a very short-lived moment of fame. Think of saliency as this roaming spotlight, it determines what we pay attention to. Specifically, the salience bias is our predisposition to pay attention to items that are more visible, distinct, and emotionally striking. We all know that feeling when we have just bought a new car and suddenly everyone on the road seems to be driving the same car, or when we have bought a pair of shoes we have been wanting for a long time and suddenly everyone seems to own that exact pair in the same color. This noticing, this "paying attention to" is saliency, and is extremely important when it comes to self-awareness. The more self-aware we are, the more we can

THE SALIENCE BIAS IS OUR PREDISPOSITION TO PAY ATTENTION TO ITEMS THAT ARE MORE VISIBLE, DISTINCT, AND EMOTIONALLY STRIKING.

identify negative, repetitive thoughts, feelings or behaviors as taking up more air time, thus becoming more salient to us. We also realize that the things that are more emotionally striking to us, that cause us to pay attention, can also be linked to things that have happened in our past (our experiences) and those people who we deemed as experts (parents, teachers, coaches, etc.). Remember, both self-awareness and salience directly influence our behavior, from a simple example of choosing a "shiny" car instead of looking at the fuel costs and the economical picture,[27] to more serious consequences involving political implications, sometimes knowing that we really do choose to see what we want to see is the most important aspect of making us aware of the whole picture.

A simple effective acronym to better understand and cultivate self-awareness is N3:

- Notice
- Name
- Narrator

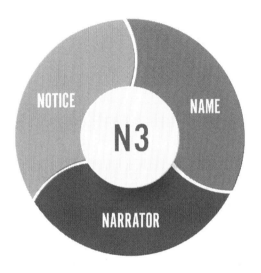

Notice: It might sound easy but most of us have forgotten to notice how we feel. The "meh" or "eh" or "fine" cloud hangs over us and for many of us; we have just become used to feeling this way. There are many ways to simply notice how you are feeling. Some people have a set time during a routine like brushing their teeth where they will just ask themselves this question. Others might practice a quick body scan while walking or driving to notice areas of tension in the body. Having played the piano growing up, I often picture the metronome. While my teacher increased the speed of the metronome, I was tasked with playing faster and faster to match its tempo. Sometimes this fast pace can feel like

ACKNOWLEDGE

our heart beats or the pace of our breathing when we are feeling anxious or stressed; maybe it's this tempo that you notice. There are many ways to approach this. Some might notice the temperature of their bodies heating up as they feel angry or frustrated, while others might be aware of the tension in their jaw, neck, or back as they enter rush hour traffic. It's not about finding the right one, it's about giving yourself permission to even ask yourself the questions: "What can I notice in my body right now? What can I notice in my breath right now? What can I notice about how I feel right now?"

The first thing is to recognize that it's there. Step back from the moment and look at the feeling. Give the feeling a name: pain, hatred, love, worry. As we discussed in Chapter 2, I believe that most of the complex emotions that we feel funnel through fear: fear of failure, fear of disappointment, fear of being judged, fear of being alone, and so on.

Name: There is enormous power in being able to name our emotions. A well-known study by Brown et al showed that individuals were only able to name three emotions they could recognize in themselves: "mad, sad, and glad."[28] Ludwig Wittgenstein, the Austrian-born philosopher, is known for saying "The limits of my language mean the limits of my world."[29] Five-time New York bestselling author Dr Brene Brown has been quoted repeating this famous line in relation to the importance of understanding emotional granularity, which is being able to differentiate between the specificity of emotions. For example, "Is what I'm feeling jealousy or envy? Do I feel angry or disappointed? Stressed or overwhelmed?" Furthermore, work by Hoemann et al[30] has shown that there is a CORRELATION between improved emotional granularity and the metric of heart rate variability through a mechanism known as respiratory sinus arrhythmia. Simply put, the better one's ability to name their emotions the better their heart rate variability (i.e., the time between heart beats), which in turn is correlated with both positive physical and mental outcomes. All of this to say that there is a link between being able to name your emotions and your actual physiology, which is incredible.

Narrator: Finally, one of the most important aspects of bolstering self-awareness is the recognition that you have an inner narrator. Alice's story demonstrates this all too well:

I was just wrapping up a patient interview with Alice, an 18 year old I knew well, when she looked at me sheepishly and said, "Is it okay if I tell you something?" The look on her face was a mixture of anxiety and apprehension. Of course I told her she could tell me anything. She disclosed that over the past few months she felt like she was hearing a voice, and it was freaking her out. When I probed more, she said the voice would come when she was walking home from school.

"It's not like somebody else's voice," she said. "But I'll be walking, carrying a big backpack stuffed full of books and clothes, and I wonder, 'Do people think I'm hiding something in my backpack?' I'll be at the grocery store, loading my cart with stuff, and I wonder, 'Are people looking at what I'm buying?' Or I'll be trying on some clothes, and I'll wonder, 'Are people judging what I'm wearing?'"

The voice told her people were laughing at her. The voice put her down, made her feel ugly, and told her she didn't belong. As we talked, we determined together that she was hearing an inner voice that sounded like someone she knew.

"Who does it sound like?" I asked.

"My mom," she said.

YOUR INNER NARRATOR

What Alice was working on there was self-awareness. Because I'd known her for several years, she summoned the courage to admit she was "hearing a voice." She wasn't becoming delusional. But the voice was still real. It was her inner narrator, someone who is constantly translating and transcribing the situations around you and comparing them to your past. Sometimes we call the voice our inner roommate. And even though many of us aren't aware that we have this narrator within us, we all have one.

You weren't born with this self-critical voice. A baby doesn't look in a mirror and say, "I'm too fat," or, "I can't do anything right." So where does this "narrator voice" come from? It comes from what I call the two "Es". The first "E" is for "experts." In most cases they aren't really experts, but they are people you perceived as authorities during your formative years, especially the first three-to-six years of your life. Those people included your parents, siblings, grandparents, uncles, aunts, teachers, coaches, church members, and so on. The experts had a huge role in shaping your self-perception.

The second "E" is for your "experiences." To explain how your brain deals with experiences, I'll describe something that just happened in my house. A bucket of water was tipped over on the stairs (don't ask how it got there). As you might imagine, the water sloshed down the stairs—not up. Water flows to its most efficient route. The water also doesn't care that it's making a mess. It chooses what's easy and efficient. Likewise, your brain also doesn't care if something it's processing is good for you or bad for you. Your brain doesn't care if you're moving ahead with your goals or standing stagnant. All it cares about is keeping you safe, and that means sticking with what's easy and familiar. As we now know, the brain loves nothing more than familiarity.

Remember, your inner narrator isn't just commenting on events that are happening with no bias. It is repeating cautions or warnings based on past experiences and what our "experts" have told us. Your brain does three things really well, without a lot of effort on your part: It cautions you, it compares you with others, and it critiques you. Think about this carefully: caution, compare, and critique.

Let me offer up an analogy a counselor once gave to me: Your inner voice is like a radio station that's always on. Although we can't necessarily prevent its content from entering our heads, we can control the volume. And, with enough practice, we can learn to change the station.

UNDERSTANDING YOUR INNER NARRATOR: THE DIVING BOARD EXERCISE

Imagine that you have climbed up to a diving board that initially seemed ok but once you got to the top appeared much higher than you expected. You want nothing more than to turn around and climb down but there is a line of swimmers waiting behind you. It's your moment to plunge into the pool. You know there's no getting out of this.

Think to yourself at that moment who in your life would be the one whispering in your ear "You got this" "You can do it." For example, maybe you were taking your college entrance exams and you heard a voice inside saying, "You've got this." Maybe it was a voice that told you, "You can open your own business," or "You can buy a house." This might be the voice of a memorable teacher, coach, parent, church leader, or counselor. These are the people who might have actually told you that they believed in you, or perhaps it wasn't the words but their behavior towards you that instilled a

YOUR INNER VOICE IS LIKE A RADIO
STATION THAT'S ALWAYS ON.
ALTHOUGH WE CAN'T NECESSARILY
PREVENT ITS CONTENT FROM
ENTERING OUR HEADS, WE
CAN CONTROL THE VOLUME.

level of trust and confidence in your underlying capability. Is there a person or experience that comes to mind?

Alternatively, is there someone that might do the opposite? Someone that might, when you were in a vulnerable and difficult position, make it feel like it was your fault? Moreover, do you remember an experience like the diving board example in which you felt trapped in some way, and you felt scared or unsure. Who did you turn to? What was their response?

This exercise is not intended to be a blame game. Don't point fingers and say, "See, Mom/Dad, if you weren't like this, I would have been happier." No, this exercise is to give us knowledge. It allows us to say, "Oh, I get it now!" It's to help you to see who you perceive to be your most important "experts."

Your previous experiences, and those you perceived as experts in your life, influence the way you see yourself, the world, and your future. According to Beck, a negative outlook in this triad (i.e., self, world, and future) can facilitate a mood disorder such as depression in the future.[31] Those with a negative self view might say things like "I always mess up." Those with a negative view on the world might feel like the world is working against them. Those with a negative view on the future might feel like they are never going to succeed.

A great example of this was seen in another patient, Hannah. Her mom is an alcoholic. As for her father, the first thing Hannah told me about him was, "My dad doesn't want me. The only reason he had me was so he could manipulate someone." Hannah now lives in foster care, in a home without other children, where the state pays a woman to take care of her, but unfortunately in her case, where there is little interaction or love.

I hadn't seen Hannah since Christmas, so I asked her how her holidays had been.

"Oh," she said, "It was blissful."

"Who did you spend it with?" I asked.

"I spent it with me, myself, and I," she said.

Here's a 14 year old spending Christmas alone, who really did feel it was "blissful." Her only experience in life had been abandonment. Her core belief regarding the world around her was that she couldn't trust others; the only person she could trust was herself. Her inner narrator reflected this as well ,and when she told me her time alone during Christmas had been "blissful" she was absolutely serious because in her mind, spending it alone with the only person she could trust (herself) was great.

Therefore if we look at that triad again above, in Hannah's case her core belief about herself was one of trust and reliance; however, about the world and possibly even the future it felt bleak and confusing.

This is how your experiences and those you perceive as experts begin to influence your inner narrator and, more specifically, how your inner narrator chooses to perceive situations related to yourself, the world around you, and your future.

YOUR FAMILY MOTTO

Did your family have a written or unwritten motto? It might have been something like, "Kids are to be seen and not heard." When growing up, my family's motto was, "Leave no stone unturned." That meant we were always supposed to keep chasing answers and driving for success. Part of that was because my parents were refugees living in a new country, so I can really understand their motivation, especially when it came to pursuing education.

A motto your family believed in doesn't have to be something your parents or your siblings could repeat back to you. It can be an implicit motto, something that you just knew, i.e., "This is what we do, and this is what we don't do." Sometimes it might not be a motto, but a set of behaviors or tendencies. I'll never forget Shannon, who came back to my office after graduating. Despite having worked together for a number of years I never realized that besides her maternal grandmother, no one in Shannon's immediate or extended family had ever graduated high school.

EVALUATE YOUR EMOTIONAL BED

Self-awareness progresses when we appreciate not only who we are, but how we feel. Remember in Chapter 1 I mentioned a term I call "emotional beds?" These are the emotions we retreat to, where we think we'll feel comfortable, where we can pull the covers over our heads and not have to explain what's going on to anyone, including ourselves. To understand the emotional bed, you need to know that emotions give you three things:

1. *They give you a sensation in your body.* Remember that even the absence of an emotion, numbness or feeling nothing, is still an emotion.

2. *They reinforce a story in your head that you believe.* That story is not false; it's true to you. But the question is, does it serve you in the short term, or does it serve you in the long term? I always say that the story you sell to yourself is delicious in the short term. It's delicious to feel resentful, frustrated, or overwhelmed. But it can be detrimental in the long term.

3. *There is usually meaning or significance within this story. Emotions give you the impression they are significant.* You feel an emotion because you value something. Otherwise, you wouldn't care.

Your emotional bed is a comfortable space—your core emotions—that you gravitate to under times of stress. As I mentioned, my default or core emotion is feeling overwhelmed. If something doesn't meet my expectations, that's the story that I sell myself in my head: "You have too many things to do. You can't possibly do everything."

Emotional beds may seem attractive, but they are a trap. When we find ourselves fleeing to our beds, we most likely will remain self-critical; we will endure recurring but needless pain. Because we are accustomed to these feelings, we may fail to look at them objectively.

Another term I use with my patients is "sticky emotions." These are feelings that emerge unbidden. They are hard to suppress, and we struggle to overcome them. It may be difficult to realize that such emotions do come and go. They don't have to last. For instance, if we feel frustration when we overeat, the process of acknowledging is to consider what pushed us to that carton of ice cream, examining the subconscious emotions that lead to the feelings without judging our actions.

"Holding on to something is a behavior as common as breathing," says psychologist Jennifer Delgado. "We tend to cling to the people we love and who play an important role in our lives. We also hold on to our most valuable possessions. To the painful memories of the past. To our social roles or to certain characteristics that we believe define us. Negative thought patterns that we have developed over time. Unrealistic hopes and expectations. Bad habits and negative emotions that make us suffer unnecessarily. What is really important is to understand the hidden meaning behind that need to retain. The key is not in what we hold onto, but in the psychological cause of that excessive attachment."[32]

In other words, when it comes to feelings, we like to hold on to what we're familiar with. We tend to hold on to those feelings even when they make us uncomfortable, unreasonable, or unpleasant. We justify our behavior because we think the feelings control us, not the other way around. To get out of your emotional bed, you first have to realize that you are lying in it. Or better yet, you need to recognize it for what it is, shake the blanket, and change the sheets.

As you evaluate your emotional bed, it's important to understand that even uncomfortable emotions—those we may deem negative—are meant to keep us safe. But once those emotions start to negatively impact our emotional health, we need to do something about them. Until that point, we need to look at them, not as things to be avoided, but as clues to investigate.

Realize also that it's possible to create a more positive emotional bed, the kind that is both reassuring and comforting.

SELF-COMPASSION IS ESSENTIAL

We have now traveled along that path I outlined, from self-awareness, over the bridge of self-acknowledgement, and now let's discuss self-love, or a term that might seem a little less indulgent: self-compassion.

One of the key questions to ask yourself to foster self compassion is "What do I need right now? Another way of thinking of this is asking yourself the question "What do I need right now that This [striving] for perfection can make us forget to take care of our basic needs, such as psychological safety, companionship, and personal creativity. Self-love is not selfish. Self-love is about acknowledging the need to work towards self-betterment. Nowadays, the definition of self-love has moved away from its traditional negative connotations such as narcissism and selfishness. It is seen as a positive psychology practice which can help people better

WHAT DO I NEED RIGHT NOW THAT THIS [STRIVING] FOR PERFECTION CAN MAKE US FORGET TO TAKE CARE OF OUR BASIC NEEDS, SUCH AS PSYCHOLOGICAL SAFETY, COMPANIONSHIP, AND PERSONAL CREATIVITY.

manage their emotions and their mental healthI'm too afraid/scared/unsure to ask for?"

"With self-compassion, we give ourselves the same kindness and care we'd give to a good friend," says Kristen Neff, PhD, of the Educational Psychology Department at the University of Texas at Austin. "Self-compassion is the process of turning compassion inward. We are kind and understanding rather than harshly self-critical when we fail, make mistakes, or feel inadequate. We give ourselves support and encouragement rather than being cold and judgmental when challenges and difficulty arise in our lives. Research indicates that self-compassion is one of the most powerful sources of coping and resilience we have available to us, radically improving our mental and physical wellbeing."

Dr. Neff is saying that we do not need to let fear of inadequacy drive us, rather we can accept our abilities and achievements as they are, and look for growth for the right reasons.[33]

Vas Touronis, a psychologist based in the United Kingdom, adds "It may sound selfish and indulgent, but (self-love) is absolutely essential to your mental health and wellbeing. And it doesn't mean you have to always [prioritize] your needs over everyone else's. If anything, having a good relationship with yourself is a selfless act. Because how you treat others is often a reflection of how you treat yourself…"

Touronis says that you can be single and happy, or in a relationship and unhappy. What really matters is your relationship with *yourself.* "Your sense of self-worth can't ever be fulfilled by external validation: it needs to come from within. Loving yourself sets the tone for the relationships you have with other people. A lack of self-love could make you a magnet for dysfunctional relationships because, when you truly love yourself, it's harder to tolerate other people treating you poorly."[34]

Dr. Kristen Neff adds, "Having self-compassion is really no different than having compassion for others. Compassion involves feeling moved by others' suffering so that your heart responds to their pain. When this occurs, you feel warmth, caring, and the desire to help the suffering person in some way. Having compassion also means that you offer understanding and kindness to others when they fail or make mistakes, rather than judging them harshly. Finally, when you feel compassion for another (rather than mere pity), it means that you realize that suffering, failure, and imperfection [are] part of the shared human experience."[35]

Self-compassion involves acting the same way towards yourself when you are having a difficult time, when you make a mistake, or when you notice something you don't like about yourself. Instead of just ignoring your pain at these times, Neff says, "Stop to tell yourself, 'this is really difficult right now.' How can I comfort and care for myself at this moment?"[36]

Instead of mercilessly criticizing and judging yourself for all your inadequacies or shortcomings, says Neff, self-compassion means you are empathic and understanding when confronted with any of your personal flaws. After all, no one ever said we were supposed to be perfect.[37]

The goal is to work on this to become more healthy and happy. Why? Because you care about yourself, not because you are worthless or unacceptable as you are. Having compassion for yourself means that you honor and accept that you are a human being. And as humans, things will not always go the way we want them to. We will encounter failures, frustrations, and losses. We have limitations, and at times we fall short of our values and ideals. The more we accept this instead of fighting against it, the more we will be able to feel compassion for ourselves and for all fellow humans on this journey of life.

Dr. Andleeb Asghar, a professional medical writer, says there is a lot of scientific evidence suggesting that self-compassion can have a positive impact on your mental health, self-esteem, and overall life satisfaction. "Modern society creates so much pressure on people—whether it's pressure to achieve status, wealth, or beauty—that it can sometimes feel easier to focus on our failures and ignore the areas where we have grown," Asghar said.[38]

I love the quote from actress Kristin Chenoweth. She says, "If you can learn to love yourself and all the flaws, you can love other people so much better. And that makes you so happy."[39]

HOW OTHERS SEE YOU

One last example in this chapter: Emma came to see me wondering if she had attention deficit hyperactivity disorder (ADHD). Like Braden, whom we discussed earlier, Emma disclosed to me that in her younger "partying" days she would often use multiple illicit street drugs. She even started combining substances to see how the mix would affect her.

She eventually became interested in the way drugs affect the body, and she started studying online and then would dive into research books and articles at the library. She learned a lot, and friends even started asking her before they experimented if it was "safe" to mix certain drugs, and where to purchase a "cleaner" supply.

As she became more aware, Emma realized how incredibly dangerous her behavior was and she began to change. When I met her, she was thankful to be in a different part of her life, although as we began to get to know one another and investigate her mental health, I could sense how much disdain she had for herself. She had been through a lot growing up, and her emotions around her experiences were firmly walled up. One day I asked her what she thought of herself, and she told me something very similar to Braden, that she loathed herself.

I pointed out to Emma how her friends, even though they were engaging in such risky behavior, turned to her to try to be as safe as they could in the moment. They sought Emma out, because they valued her opinion and knew she cared. I pointed out that her friends essentially trusted her with their lives.

I'll never forget how Emma looked at me. It was like for the first time she saw herself as her friends did—as someone trying to keep them safe despite the incredible risks they were taking. Emma had learned not to give much away in her expression, but there was a flicker of a smile and a small nod of her head. She said, "I never thought about it that way."

The exercise I then went through with Emma is called view-pointing. It's a cognitive behavioral technique, or CBT. Here's how it works: Say you're really focused on a problem. You have a bunch of complex emotions going on. Ask yourself, "What would your best friend say in this situation right now? How would they handle things with you, what would they say to you?" Or better yet, "What advice would you give to your spouse, friend, or sibling if they were in a similar situation?" Viewpointing takes you out of the fire. It allows you to step back and consider.

This, of course, can be hard when you are in the midst of internal turmoil. To create perspective, you need space. We all love to faceplant ourselves in our problems. We do it all the time. But to be objective, we need to separate ourselves from our problems. Viewpointing allows us to step back and consider, "What would somebody who loves me say in this situation?" or "What would you say to somebody else you care about?"

Consider who turns to you for advice and who you turn to. How have you have shown up for others in the past? What counsel has worked, and what would they say to you today?

One of the great things about viewpointing is that it allows us to not only look at what has happened to us previously, including improvements we've made, but also to acknowledge what is happening to us right now. Viewpointing allows us to see our emotions for what they are, and then to see beyond our own emotions.

BENEFITS OF SELF-COMPASSION

We have many people in our society who can't appreciate their contributions and worth. It's why happiness for many people seems to be long-gone as well. It doesn't have to be that way.

We need to be more self-aware and acknowledge what we are feeling. We start with the idea of all the basic and the complex emotions that tumble into the funnel of our emotions, including recognizing how fear ends up being at the base of the funnel for most of us. We then become aware of our inner narrator, whose voice comes from experts and experiences. And then, now that you acknowledge that voice in your head, the question becomes: what do you do with that feeling?

If you are like me and default to feeling overwhelmed, you ask yourself: "Do I want to stay overwhelmed, or do I want to shift?" If your answer is that you want to shift, it's time to think of self-compassion as a tool you can use. You cannot change your emotions like you change your clothes. It does not happen that easily or that fast. Instead, what if I told you that the best way to change your emotions is to soften them?

We all know that feeling of cutting through butter left on the counter compared to when it's in the fridge. On the counter the butter is soft, smooth, almost silky as you cut through it.

Self compassion allows you to soften your emotions, and that's a good thing.

CHAPTER 5

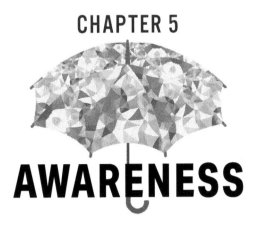

AWARENESS

STOP LABELING EMOTIONS AS GOOD OR BAD.

Many of us have an innate sense early on that emotions are either good or bad. We have learned from earlier chapters that this is far from true. We also know that our brain works based on past experience and that it prefers that which is familiar and comfortable.

Consider what happened one morning when I made instant oatmeal for my son's breakfast. He took his first bite and told me it was too cold. So, I popped it in the microwave and pressed "quick minute" even though I knew it probably only needed 10 more seconds to get warm. I was cleaning up a spill of some sort, and the other 50 seconds rushed by. I knew before I gave the oatmeal back to him that he would say: "Now it's too hot!" He also told me, in rapid succession, that the oatmeal was too dry and not sweet enough.

"Can I just have pancakes instead?" he said.

Like my son, many of us seem to live with a Goldilocks view of the world. We want things to be just right—not too hot, not too cold. This viewpoint is especially widespread when it comes to our mental health. We tend to define mental health as the absence of distress or the presence of happiness. We say, "I am happy, joyful, and bubbly, so my mental health must be all right."

But what happens when things don't go our way? If someone cuts me off in traffic, literally or figuratively, and I feel unhappy, angry, or vengeful, does that automatically mean I'm not mentally healthy?

> MANY OF US SEEM TO LIVE WITH A GOLDILOCKS VIEW OF THE WORLD. WE WANT THINGS TO BE JUST RIGHT—NOT TOO HOT, NOT TOO COLD.

CLUES, NOT TRUTHS

Part of feeling better is understanding that we don't need to justify our emotions. They just happen. If we feel something we don't like, such as envy or jealousy, it's counterproductive to say, "I shouldn't feel that way." We just feel it. We are not evil for feeling that way. It's what we do in response to the emotions that counts, and sometimes this action can simply be acknowledging the emotion in the first place.

Emotions are clues, not truths. Mental health is not about avoiding emotions or focusing only on happy feelings. Mental health involves learning proper ways to respond to uncomfortable—even painful—experiences and the resulting emotions. We are mentally healthy when we experience the full range of human emotions, both positive and negative, and deal with them in appropriate ways.

Mental health means learning to accept that all our emotions—ups and downs, comfortable emotions, and uncomfortable ones—are temporary. When we have negative or unproductive feelings, it's contrary to our mental health to hold on to those feelings. It's when these emotions become sticky that we run into problems.

In this chapter, we'll learn what we have control over and what we don't. Briefly, what's in our control is the story we tell ourselves about what's going on.

COMFORTABLE BLANKETS

We have talked about your emotional bed. Let me draw on this analogy to understand how we can accept the uncomfortable feelings we have.

You know how you feel lying in bed on Monday morning after a nice long weekend. Your covers are warm, with just the right hint of coolness as you slip your hand beneath your pillow. It's dark and cold outside and that makes the coziness of your bed even more inviting. We have all felt this pull toward the comfort of our bed, regardless of the outside forces. Breaking the inertia seems almost impossible. Then the alarm sounds! Its unwelcome audio slapping you back to reality.

Feelings we aren't accustomed to are like that alarm. Remember, your brain craves what is familiar. Its priority is not to keep you happy or healthy, it is to find familiarity because that is where it believes it can keep you the safest. Familiarity is your brain's comfort blanket, even if those emotions are not necessarily healthy (think of my default to feeling overwhelmed).

The concept of the emotional bed came to me when I found myself crawling into my emotional blankets: "I'm overwhelmed." "I'm frustrated." "I'm afraid." I did it again and again. Every time I found myself stressed, every time something didn't go the way I had planned, or the kids didn't act the way I wanted, the jump from the stimulus (i.e., child has a tantrum) to emotion (feeling overwhelmed) became quicker and more seamless.

When I allowed myself to be more self-aware, I found what I was doing fascinating. First, because I was able to discover my default emotion. Second, because I realized that, unlike the popular belief that "uncomfortable" emotions are bad for us, or that we don't like uncomfortable emotions, we are in fact adept at feeling them because they are familiar to us.

Surrounding myself with the comforter of, "I'm overwhelmed," became easy, predictable, and familiar. It became my emotional bed. We all have an emotional bed, whether we like to admit it or not. Being self-aware means being able to identify our bed for what it is.

To learn what emotions we have control over and how we can accept what we might not be able to change, several key pieces that make up your emotional bed that we need to examine:

DEFAULT EMOTIONS
TYPICAL TRIGGERS
YOUR INTERNAL STORYLINE
YOUR REACTIONS

DEFAULT EMOTIONS

"During difficult times, we often find ourselves defaulting to a single, dominant emotion, even when another might be more 'logical,'says science writer Rachel Fairbank. "For example, your default emotion may be anxiety, which is what you'll feel during stressful times, even if a more appropriate emotional reaction might be anger, sadness, or frustration…"[40]

We prefer our dominant emotion since that's familiar to us and what we know the best. However, it's important to experience a range of emotions, as this leads to a more healthy, fulfilling life.

"One way to think about emotions is to think about all of the different emotions as being part of a balanced ecosystem," Fairbank said. "Within an ecosystem there are many different components, all of which are important for a healthy system. If this balance gets disrupted though, with one emotion becoming heavily dominant, then the overall health of the system gets thrown off balance. As studies are showing, people who experience a broad range of emotions tend to have better mental and physical health…"[41]

Emotions all have a purpose, explains Alice Boyes, PhD. "In fact, they all have useful purposes. However, each of us has our own emotional style. We're predisposed to feel some emotions more strongly and more easily than others. Many of us have one single emotion that's dominant. It's the emotion we jump to feeling when situations are difficult. When you understand how your emotions work, you can manipulate them. This can be useful when you're feeling burnt out from one particular emotion."[42]

No one emotion is better than any other, but too much of any specific emotion isn't good for us. Even too much happiness can be an impediment to overall mental health. Why? Because any dominant emotion leaves no room for other emotions that are actually useful.

"Your less dominant emotions might be painful to feel, but they're also helpful. Or at least they can be if you channel them correctly," Boyes said. "If you always see the world through the lens of your dominant emotion, you'll make incorrect and incomplete interpretations of situations. Your decision-making will be worse."[43]

She encourages you to let yourself sit with your non-dominant emotions for a few seconds or a few minutes. Let them exist without pushing or pulling them, and without analyzing them.

"What works for me in reducing anxiety is to let those other emotions, like grief and sadness, surface more," she added. "The more I allow myself to feel those feelings, the more I get a 'break' from feeling anxious."[44]

EMOTIONAL TRIGGERS

An emotional trigger is anything that can create an emotional reaction. It could be an experience, a smell, a sight, a rejection or betrayal, challenged beliefs, loss of control, or being excluded or ignored. Anything that brings about a specific, overwhelming emotion—all despite your current mood—can be a trigger

Writer Crystal Raypole notes that emotional triggers vary from person to person, but could include things such as unwanted memories, uncomfortable topics, or another person's words or actions, etc.

Raypole says, "On any given day, you probably experience a range of emotions —excitement, unease, frustration, joy, disappointment. These often relate to specific events, such as meeting with your boss, talking about current events with a friend, or seeing your partner. Your response to these events can vary based on your frame of mind and the circumstances surrounding the situation." [45] Your response will also vary based on your emotional bed.

"When strong emotions come up, don't try to ignore them or fight them back," she said. "Instead, approach them with curiosity to get more insight on what may have triggered them. Do any patterns stand out?" [46]

She also notes that triggers can evoke plenty of emotions, which is normal. But before you can begin working through them, you have to accept them. Your emotional bed makes it easier to avoid dealing with these kinds of emotions. However, denying or ignoring what you feel generally only makes it worse over time.

Explore how your thoughts trigger your reaction, say Dr. Joti Samra and Mary Ann Banton of the Workplace Strategies team. "Choose one of your emotional triggers. Yes, most of us have more than one! Think about your usual reaction to that trigger – anger, pity, sadness, shame, guilt, defensiveness, hostility, frustration, overwhelm, fear or something else. Now think about the thoughts and memories attached to that trigger."

"Once you've identified your most frequent emotional triggers and explored the thoughts or memories you relate to that trigger, you're ready to choose your reaction. Rather than giving into the trigger, recognize that you can control your thoughts and memories. You can then look objectively at the current situation and choose a healthier or more appropriate reaction. This doesn't mean you won't always be triggered. But, you can avoid letting the trigger dictate your behaviors and words."

The authors suggest the next time you feel any emotional reaction:

- Ask yourself if you've been triggered.
- Identify the thoughts and memories that influenced your reaction.

- Consider how you can respond appropriately to the current situation.[47]

Raypole suggests these strategies for identifying and coping with triggers:

- *Own your feelings.* It's okay to feel whatever we are feeling at that moment.
- *Give yourself some space.* Give yourself a chance to cool off so you can handle the situation more productively then return to the situation with a clearer head.
- *Communicate.* Try using I-statements and other healthy communication skills to address the situation.
- *Identify toxic relationship patterns.* People who seem to want to push your buttons intentionally will often continue doing so, no matter how many times you ask them to stop.
- *Keep a mood journal.* Regularly tracking your emotions in a journal can help you recognize specific patterns, such as emotional triggers and times of greater vulnerability.[48]

YOUR INTERNAL STORYLINE

In Chapter 4 we talked about your inner narrator, the voice you hear based on those you considered experts during your formative years and also based on your experiences in life.

When I was a girl, we would cover a hot kettle of soup with Saran Wrap. This kept the soup hot—sometimes too hot. To cool the soup down, we would poke holes in the plastic film and let the heat vent. Now, think of a story you're telling yourself in your head, and then vent it by poking holes in it: (Poke) "Is there evidence to disprove this story?" (Poke) "Is it reasonable that this situation will never change?"

This way, even as you're dealing with a problem, you're asking yourself the questions: "Is it permanent? "Is it pervasive?" "Is it in every aspect of my life?" Of course, the answer to these questions is most often "No." But here's a real good hole-poker: "Have I solved harder problems than this before?" Most of the time, the answer to that question is "Yes."

By cooling the soup, so to speak, you give yourself the freedom to step back, think more clearly, and act rather than react.

Research shows that stories shape us. "Stories that turn out well may give people the hope they need to live productive lives," says Sadie F. Dingfelder, writing for the American Psychological Association. "And stories that vividly describe turmoil seem to help people grow wiser in the aftermath of major life challenges."[49]

The power of narrative, however, isn't always positive. John Holmes, PhD, a psychology professor at Waterloo University, says telling yourself stories that focus on negative traits can cause you to forget about the positive traits you used to cherish. In other words, if our inner narrator is constantly focusing on the negative, we will default to our fears, weaknesses, and failures rather than cheering ourselves on to success.

Holmes adds, "For better or worse, stories are a very powerful source of self-persuasion."[50]

Dan McAdams, PhD, a psychology professor at Northwestern University has spent years studying stories. He said, "Stories help us smooth out some of the decisions we have made and create something that is meaningful and sensible out of the chaos of our lives." Stories are the best way to make sense of complex problems.[51]

Dingfelder summarizes: "Taken together, psychologists' narrative research makes one resounding point: We don't just tell stories, stories tell us. They shape our thoughts and memories, and even change how we live our lives."[52]

YOUR REACTION

So, you've figured out your default emotion; you've learned to recognize your emotional triggers, and you know the internal storyline you're most likely to tell yourself. What now? How do you react?

The way we react to our emotional triggers and our internal narrator is often funneled through our defense mechanisms. There are both healthy and unhealthy defense mechanisms, and many of us have adopted a playlist of both types. Healthy defense mechanisms would be things like sublimation, i.e. taking an uncomfortable emotion like anger and channeling it into your next workout. Common—and likely less healthy—defense mechanisms I often see are:

- *Suppression: Pushing the emotion as deep as it can go. Often Netflix, wine or a combination of both are involved*
- *Blaming: It's not my fault I feel this way, it's because of "x" or "y."*
- *Denial: Simply ignoring there is an issue in the first place. A version of this could involve someone struggling with substance abuse continuing to go to work as they refuse to believe they are struggling.*

Remember: It's important not to get down on yourself for having emotions or feelings, but it's worthwhile looking at practices to shift the emotions that rise in situations that often bring you back to your emotional bed.

QUESTIONS IN THE SHADOWS

Perhaps the most important reason to understand why we retreat to our emotional beds is to find answers to questions that lurk in the shadows: "What situation brought about a retreat to my emotional bed?" "What feeling am I trying to hide or escape from in my emotional bed?" It's like pulling on a thread, and one question leads to another: "What do I not want to deal with?" "What would that say about me?"

Let me give a personal example. As a little girl I placed motherhood on a pedestal. Watching home videos of my sister and me playing quietly, with soft music in the background while we munched the healthy snacks our mother had prepared for us, I romanticized motherhood as carefree and, dare I say, easy. However, when I became a mother I found out all too soon that "easy" would never be a word to describe my pregnancy, postpartum, and motherhood journey.

I just wanted to be a good mom. So, when my baby began losing weight or was waking up every 45 minutes at night, my inner narrator was pointing the finger of blame at me. My deepest fear, I discovered, was that I might learn I didn't enjoy being a mother, that this fantasy land of rainbows, unicorns, and wet wipes was simply not my cup of tea. But instead of accepting those emotions, I defaulted to guilt (part of my emotional bed). For me, guilt was more familiar, tolerable, and safer than the reality of the situation.

Well, it's three kids later now, and guess what I found—albeit the hard way? Not everyone—in fact maybe no one—likes being a parent *all the time*. Often it *is* hard, sometimes it *is* thankless, and at the best of times, it *is* unpredictable. But it is also magical, funny, and rewarding when you least expect it.

FEAR IN DISGUISE

While any emotion can be unfamiliar and lead us to our emotional bed, one of the most common is fear. So, let's double-click on the fears I revealed in myself as I dug deeper: fear of not liking motherhood, fear of not being good enough, fear of failure. When these fears arise, I feel stress. And stress comes from wanting, or even more precisely, *expecting* things to be different than they are. At such times, feeling overwhelmed is a big part of my emotional bed. If the kids are fighting, yelling, or doing both at the same time, if I'm loaded with work and also trying to clean the house, or if I just haven't had time to relax, no matter how I try to solve my emotional equation, it always equals "overwhelmed."

> **WHILE ANY EMOTION CAN BE UNFAMILIAR AND LEAD US TO OUR EMOTIONAL BED, ONE OF THE MOST COMMON IS FEAR.**

To identify the specific fears that may be sending us to our emotional beds, try this exercise:

- *Identify an emotion that is common for you:* It could be anger, frustration, hopelessness, sadness, etc. Remember, even numbness counts as an emotion.
- *Ask: "What does this feel like in my body? How do I know I am feeling this way?*
- *Determine what triggers this emotion:* For example, "I feel this way when something doesn't go the way I hoped or planned."
- *Ask: "What does the trigger say about me?"* Don't just ask yourself once, ask yourself the same question several times.

Go back to the seven-layers-deep exercise and the list of common fears to see, as you keep asking yourself "What would that say about me?" You can get closer to identifying your underlying fear. A great example of this might be someone who shies away from opportunities. When a new opportunity presents itself, instead of being met by optimism, they feel overwhelmed, even anxious. If the trigger is a new opportunity (think applying for a new job) the emotion would be anxiety, overwhelm and self -doubt. A good strategy to keep asking the "What would that say about you" question is asking yourself "What if you didn't get the job?" Perhaps the seven-layers-deep exercise would look something like this:

I knew I wasn't going to get the job.
I wasn't smart enough.
I didn't put myself out there enough.
I need more experience in the field to put myself out there.
I am not as qualified as the other candidates so why even bother.
I don't think I can ever be as good as those other candidates.
Underlying fear: Fear of not being good enough

Think of these questions like wringing out a dishcloth. Sometimes you need that extra squeeze to get all the water out. This is where giving yourself the permission to ask the hard questions is crucial. This is where being curious and not critical or self condemning is essential. This is the start of how we feel better.

I love this analogy: "Your fears are like bowling pins. Your job in life is to knock them down one by one" because the truth of the matter is that the same fears we have keep showing up in different

YOUR FEARS ARE LIKE BOWLING PINS. YOUR JOB IN LIFE IS TO KNOCK THEM DOWN ONE BY ONE ways in our everyday lives. Our fear of failure denies us from taking on that leadership position; it stops us from trying to learn a new skill, and it holds us back when our relationships are no longer serving us. It is all the same fear, it just wears a different costume.

STICKY EMOTIONS

I love many things about working with adolescents. One is their brutal and refreshing sense of honesty. Another is how they come up with phrases of brilliant wisdom at times when you weren't sure they were listening to you.

One such moment came when I was speaking to a patient who had started a low dose of antidepressant medication as well as engaging in regular counseling. Instead of the usual answers like "Okay," "Good," or "I'm not sure yet," she said, "My thoughts are just not as sticky as they used to be."

"Sticky?" Why hadn't I thought of that! Of course, some thoughts are sticky! Think of the time you got into a fight with your partner or felt misunderstood by a friend. There is a Velcro-like effect to the thoughts and the feelings. You can't stop yourself from running and re-running certain scenarios in your head.

Such stories become glued in our head. Our internal narrator convinces us to believe them. And this presents a paradox behind emotional insight: As much as you want to feel *all* of your emotions and feelings, like the colors on a color wheel, you also want to create space between yourself and your feelings so that you can *witness* them, rather than being whisked away by them. And that's hard to do when you feel stuck in a certain line of believing or thinking. It's when these sticky emotions become comfortable to us that they become our emotional bed.

This is where the principles you're learning in *Feel Better* come into play. This book presents thoughts, tools, and techniques, not only to help you to recognize and accept feelings and emotions, but to enable you to reshape the inner narrative and move toward hearing an inner voice that says, "You are capable of good things. You can and will do them."

CHAPTER 6

ACCEPT

CHOOSE WHICH EMOTIONS TO ANALYZE AND WHICH TO LET GO.

When I was young, my dad taught me to play tennis. One day, as I was running all over the court chasing his serves, lobs, and volleys, I realized my dad wasn't even breaking a sweat, while I was about to drop. He stopped playing for a minute and we sat courtside. He taught me a great lesson in a few words: "Some of these shots I'm sending to you are crap, but you're chasing them anyway. Stop it."

It was more than a good tennis lesson: It was a great life lesson. *Each of us has emotions served to us every day, but many of those emotions aren't worth chasing. In this chapter, we will analyze emotions to identify those that are worth chasing, and those to let go.*

THINK BETTER ABOUT EMOTIONS

Let's say right off the bat that we're not labeling emotions as good or bad. It's the actions we take based on the emotions that can be good or bad.

"Emotions are often categorized into either good or bad and there is often also a judgment based on the label given," says an article by Symmetry Counseling. "Typically, such emotions as anger, jealousy, sadness, or frustration are considered 'bad,' while emotions such as happiness, joy, love, or excitement are considered 'good.' However, we are doing ourselves a huge injustice by categorizing emotions. Emotions are not good or bad, they just are. For the most part, our emotions are an automatic reaction, something we have little control over or can stop from happening. Emotions help us to understand ourselves and situations, make decisions, and often play a large part in our behaviors, actions, and interactions with others."[53]

The fact is, all emotions are okay and need to be felt, it is the reaction or behavior that comes from those emotions that can be considered "good" or "bad," or "healthy" or "unhealthy." Emotions happen and are typically out of our control, but what is in our control is their impact on us: the way we react to them, and how we, in turn, behave or act due to our emotions.

"Emotions help us to communicate with others, such as when we feel sad and need some help," says Emily Bucher, a psychotherapist at the Ohio State University. "They can also help us to act quickly in important situations. For example, when you're about to cross the street and see a car coming quickly, fear gets you to jump back onto the curb. Emotions also provide important information and can sometimes be experienced as a 'gut feeling' or intuition. The simple act of labeling what you're feeling can help regulate your emotions. Emotions come and go like waves if we let them. The idea here is to ride the wave of emotion instead of trying to stop a giant wave and getting pushed around."[54]

Kendra Cherry, a psychosocial rehabilitation specialist, says, "Emotions play a critical role in how we live our lives, from influencing how we engage with others in our day to day lives to affecting the decisions we make. By understanding some of the different types of emotions, you can gain a deeper understanding of how these emotions are expressed and the impact they have on your behavior."[55]

She added, "It is important to remember, however, that no emotion is an island. Instead, the many emotions you experience are nuanced and complex, working together to create the rich and varied fabric of your emotional life."[56]

ORGANIZE YOUR EMOTIONS

Brianna Wiest, who covers stories on emotional intelligence and millennial trends for *Forbes*, says, "People who are controlled by their emotions typically have something in common: they tend to only do what feels most comfortable." They miss the fact that some uncomfortable emotions are doing us good.

"Processing trauma doesn't feel good but it does good. Procrastinating feels good but it doesn't do good. The same logic applies to so many things: eating a healthy lunch, heading into the gym for a workout, calling your mother. If you let feelings control your actions, you will never progress in life. You will wonder why you keep circling the same patterns, habits, and unhealthy relationships."[57]

She continues: "By organizing your emotions, you are placing them in a context. You are figuring out where they come from, whether or not they serve you, and what they are trying to tell you."

Wiest suggests three ways to start organizing:

1. **MAKE A LIST OF YOUR FEELINGS.** Describe to yourself the various feelings and thoughts you are having. It's normal if some are contradictory. Wiest suggests your list may look like this: "I feel really exhausted and drained today, and I don't feel like going to work." Then also: "I feel excited about completing that big project, and for my weekend trip coming up. I want to have my work done before then."

2. **STRUCTURE YOUR DAY TO HONOR YOUR NEEDS.** Too often, people live by an unrealistic all-or-nothing mentality. If someone feels burned out, they'll think they need a vacation. If they feel inspired, they'll think they need to power through the next 12 hours without a break. Neither is a sustainable solution. Instead, try structuring your day expecting to accomplish a little less when you need to. Or maybe you'll be able to accomplish a little more when you're inspired.

3. **CREATE A "TO WORRY ABOUT" LIST.** Wiest suggests we jot down anything and everything that comes up in our day that's bothering us. Then we should designate a time to sit down and review the list. When you do, you'll realize most of it was nonsense that came and went. However, there will be a few important points that require your attention.

Make an action plan to address or resolve what's bothering you. Wiest suggests you'll gain confidence by addressing what's weighing on you and realizing how some of your worries might not be as pressing as you thought at the time.[58]

AN UNFORGETTABLE MOMENT

There are some moments as a clinician that you never forget. One of these happened for me on a spring day. It involved a spider. I was speaking with Christina, a 16-year-old patient I had met several times. Over the previous visits we had discussed everything from her abuse of substances to her need to be tested for sexually transmitted diseases. I could see that some of the choices she was making—whether they were related to what she ingested or some poor relationships—were becoming more risky as she continued to hang out with a crowd that considered such things normal.

As we dove into some of these sensitive topics, I suddenly noticed that above her head, crawling aimlessly across the wall, was a rather large spider. Few things can disrupt my concentration when a patient is opening up to me, but I have a great fear of spiders. And on this occasion, that fear took control.

Christina sensed my fear. She followed my gaze to the spider. "Do you want me to take care of it?" she said. Relieved, I handed her a tissue. She responded with a look of irritation I still remember. She said, "I don't kill things. Do you have a cup I can use to catch it?"

Fortunately, I had some paper cups in my office. Christina used one to scoop the spider up. Then she deposited it outside. We resumed our conversation. But long after she left, that experience with Christina and the spider remained in my mind. On one hand, here was a young adolescent making hazardous decisions that compromised values she held about her personal safety. Yet, when it came to dealing with a tiny arachnid, she was steadfast in her beliefs and thoughts toward animals and killing a creature of any kind. Interesting.

Emotions *can*, in fact, teach us many things. Like me in that meeting, emotions can direct our focus toward items that need our attention (like spiders). They influence both our social and physical health. And they even help with our creativity and performance. Emotions can do all of these things because they act as a compass, directing us toward what we care about and value. In Christina's value system, caring for living creatures and doing them no harm was written in permanent marker.

One of our jobs as teachers and parents is to help our kids find and refine their value systems. A clear, but often missed opportunity to do this is to underline strong values when you see them. For example, when Christina came back from taking the spider outside, I said, "It seems like you care about animals." She then told me how she recently became a vegetarian, which has caused her to have a deeper respect for all life. She went on to tell me how she wanted to become a veterinary assistant. The interesting part was when I framed her current decisions as potentially derailing her future goal- ie what she truly valued - it was then and only then that she started listening.

I remember a time when I was out with my husband, kids, and my parents in a restaurant. The kids were misbehaving, and by the time we left I was horribly upset. But as I processed what I was feeling, I wasn't sure what was driving the emotion. Of course, I was frustrated with my children's behavior, especially their tantrums. And I was tired of cleaning up their messes—spilled ketchup, napkins on the floor, food played with but left on the plate.

But frankly, they are three boys. We've been through this kind of stuff before (lots). There had to be something more going on.

After some analysis, I figured out what it was. I wasn't angry; I was embarrassed. I care a lot about what my parents think of me and of my parenting, and I found it hard to struggle so much in front of them. By using my emotions as a compass, I came to understand that what I wanted was to please my parents and to gain their approval. I also realized that I needed to give myself credit for dealing with unruly children in a public setting, and that many mothers struggle with the same thing. Later that day, I even reminisced with my mother and father about when I shoved a green pea up my nose (unfortunately a true story) "And you turned out alright," my father said, laughing.

Remember: Emotions are a compass. It's your job to follow the arrow. Following the arrow takes self-awareness. And being self-aware means you need to practice self-acknowledgement and self-compassion.

VALUES VERSUS IDENTITY

Consider this phrase: You don't tend to have a strong emotional reaction to something unless you care about it. For example, if you don't care about being a team player, if you don't care about how you are perceived by your colleagues, then walking in late to a meeting or turning in a project after its deadline might not affect you much emotionally. But because you do care, you allow your emotional compass to guide you toward effective performance in the workplace.

When you go to a dinner party or social event where you meet new people, one of the first things you do is to find a way to introduce yourself. Often, the anchor point of such a conversation is

EMOTIONS ARE A COMPASS. IT'S YOUR JOB TO FOLLOW THE ARROW. FOLLOWING THE ARROW TAKES SELF-AWARENESS. AND BEING SELF-AWARE MEANS YOU NEED TO PRACTICE SELF-ACKNOWLEDGEMENT AND SELF-COMPASSION.

personal identity—your profession, the title you hold, where you work, and whether you have kids.

One day I accompanied my son to his friend's birthday party. Rambunctious kindergarten students filled the room, surrounded by tired parents sipping coffee and making small talk. Not knowing anyone, I found myself alone for a while until two parents wandered over. We discussed life with young kids. Then I found myself steering the conversation toward my profession. I told them, not so subtly, about something that happened "in the clinic." This would set them up to ask what my job was. They played along and I was able to tell them, yes, I was a doctor. I found myself standing taller and feeling more confident. I was on an invisible pedestal created by society.

Although I feel somewhat embarrassed thinking back on that conversation, I want to share what happened as I went home. Instead of purging my memory of the event (I really wanted to), I decided to implement what I tell my patients to do: be curious rather than self-critical. My analysis showed that the reason I had decided to point them toward the "MD" behind my name was simple: I wanted acceptance. I wanted to feel like I mattered, to feel that despite being brown, short, and not looking like most moms at the school, I deserved to belong.

Until I entered the world of emotional literacy, I had never thought much about my value system. I grew up in a very identity-centric universe where credentials, accolades, and the alphabet behind your name mattered. I have since learned that our identities are flexible. They don't define us. It is our value systems that are foundational.

The first time I worked at the Youth Health Centre (now called the Foundry) in Abbotsford, BC I remember feeling extremely uncomfortable. I was intimidated by teenagers, especially those that acted and looked the way these teenage patients often did.

When I was growing up, I intrinsically felt the need to cross the road if I ever saw a teenager who looked like the patients I was now treating. This predisposition had obviously followed me into adulthood.

But I had a mentor who helped me see the need to change my perception. I quickly realized what these adolescents often needed was not just physical, but social and emotional support as well. They needed help with housing, with food, and with social skills. They needed the advocacy of someone who believed in them. And they needed their own agency, based on the knowledge that we trusted them.

When I was in medical school, I never would have imagined that I would enter this kind of work, but I found myself loving it. I loved it because I worked with those who truly needed help, who were marginalized, but who still had such a big, beautiful life ahead of them.

Now I value working with marginalized populations and helping those who feel they are on the outskirts of society. In addition to counseling, you will often find me with my patients demonstrating stretches or exercises for their physical aches and pains because many of them cannot afford physiotherapy. I love being able to get to the root of their health issues. I simply love this work.

It has taken me a long time to tease apart the threads of my identity and my value system. Remember: your identity is flexible. Who you are today and who you are five years from now might be radically different. But your values are firm—they are what you build from.

Try this exercise:

EXERCISE: IDENTITY AND VALUE SYSTEM

THE DINNER PARTY TEST

I call this the dinner party test because I have used it as a meaningful way to entertain friends who come to spend an evening with us. Try it for yourself. There are no right or wrong answers. All of us will use our identity as an anchor point, especially in unfamiliar situations. The magic happens when we can link our value systems into the conversation. Here's how the test works.

If you had to introduce yourself to strangers, what would be the first thing you would say to describe yourself? Draw two columns: one with "Identity" as a header and the other with "Value System" as a header. In the first column, write down all the things that make up your identity. Examples for me might be:

IDENTITY

- Wife
- Mother
- Doctor
- Volunteer
- Author and speaker

Now in the second column, write down a list of your values, or at least your top five values. This is *much* harder to do. Remember, things you value can be things that you care deeply about and/or things that really fire you up. If you have a reaction when something is mentioned, it's likely that buried in your well of emotions is something you care about and value. Here is an attempt at my list:

VALUES

- I value family above all else.
- I value food and exercise as medicine.
- I value working with marginalized populations.
- I value community and social connections.
- I value mental health.

Create your own list of values and keep going if you can. Writing down all the things you care about can help immensely when you are trying to develop a sense of emotions that are worthy of chasing. As your list of values takes shape, ask yourself this question:

Whose values are these (mine, my parents, my partner's, etc.)?

Often, especially when we are young, we take on the value system of those we deem as experts simply to gain acceptance. Take this opportunity to evaluate your list, asking yourself sincerely, "What do I care about?" Not "What do my parents care about?" not "What does my partner care about?" not my boss, not my friends. "What do *I* care about?"

Now, rank the subjective importance of each value.

When I ask people to take this test, it isn't uncommon for me to see on people's list's something like, "I value family," or, "I value spending time with my kids." These are wonderful. But now comes a significant part of the test: Reflect on the question: How much time do you actually spend on these things?

Remember: your checks, credit card statements, and calendar don't lie. Are you spending your time on the things you value? Sometimes we have necessary obligations, such as working to pay the bills. But that's different. That's an obligation, a necessity. Here, we are talking about when you have a choice where to spend your time and whether this is in true alignment with what you care about most.

Now that you've completed the test, what do you do with the results? Remember, the purpose of the test is to help you align the roles you play and the time you spend with the values you hold most dear.

I find having a solid understanding of which values we hold closest gives some reference to how to interpret our emotional clues. If emotions are a compass, our values are our map. To get a better sense of the direction your compass is pointing, make a list of your most common, recurring emotions you experience in a given week. For me this list could include:

COMMON EMOTIONS

- Overwhelmed
- Embarrassed
- Loved
- Guilty
- Happy

Compare your lists of values and common emotions. For example, I play the role of wife and mother because I value family above all else. I spend a lot of time and money on my family. So when I feel overwhelmed, is that emotion leading me toward furthering my value of "family above all else?" How can I let feeling loved and happy guide me toward that value? How can I let those emotions guide me to furthering my main values?

Let's return to my tennis analogy. Is feeling loved and happy a shot worth running after? I think so. Is feeling overwhelmed worth pursuing, or should I show myself some compassion and let it go? I've found with my patients that if we lean into more of what we value instead of the emotions we experience, the emotions that seem overwhelming can become less so.

FINDING PURPOSE

I've talked to thousands of people, including patients and audience members at various seminars and talks I have given. Many are going through a difficult time, overwhelmed by things that seem totally beyond their control. Illness and health-related problems, for example, are often all-consuming. I often ask them these questions: What do you care about? What brings you joy? What gets you fired up? Many find it hard to answer because they don't think about these things often, especially when preoccupied with challenges.

Often, we find ourselves in a loop of work, home, bed, repeat. Perhaps one of the most valuable gifts we can give ourselves in life is to retrofit our work to something we value. I get it; not all of us can choose our occupation or how we earn a living. However, is there something in your daily activities that you can tie to something you love and care for? In the same way, can you use a value system to help move you toward a goal that you are having difficulty accomplishing?

Whenever my boys ask me "Which one of us do you love more?" I'll laugh and say, "The answer is hidden in a treasure box somewhere in the world; the only problem is that you don't have a map." Joking aside, I feel that we live in a society that tends to picture our life's purpose in the same way. We feel that somewhere in our 20s we need to "find" this mysterious purpose; as if there is just one purpose for each person and you are not "complete" until you have found it—much like my treasure box analogy.

Is it possible that we start living our life WITH PURPOSE rather than FOR a specific purpose?

In an article in *Harvard Business Review*, writer Rebecca Knight quotes Necla Keleş, a professor in the Department of Organizational Management at Bahçeşehir University: "Nothing gives you more energy than a clear purpose," Keleş says. Without one, "even just getting out of bed every morning becomes a challenge."[59]

Knight also quotes Karen Dillon, Clayton Christensen, and James Allworth who co-authored the bestseller *How Will You Measure Your Life?* The authors say, "Luckily, reengaging with your job and reminding yourself of 'who you are and why you do what you do' doesn't necessarily require a grand gesture or journey. There are many different ways you can find purpose."[60]

The authors then summarize a list of suggestions that are far from "grand" but which allow us move towards cultivating a life of more meaning:

Offset negativity. Just as micro-stresses eat away at you, micro-moments of pleasure can help you find your way back, they say. Look for ways to feel good and uplifted: Read about real-life heroes, take a nature walk, attend a religious service, page through an art book, or scroll through photographs of faraway places. And take a break from the constant negativity of news programs.

Cultivate humility. People are going through difficulties all over the world. The authors say: "Have compassion. Seek reminders that you're not alone and that you're connected to bigger things." It may sound corny, but practicing gratitude provides a pathway to positive emotions that can neutralize the challenges you inevitably experience.

Reflect on your values. The authors also recommend reflecting on what you care about and what motivates you. "Finding meaning in your work requires thinking about how you're living your life—how you're spending your time and how you're using your abilities," they add. You don't need to cure diseases or save endangered species for your work to be meaningful. The authors recommend asking colleagues and members of your team: "How is what we do helping people and making the world better? Why does our work matter right now?" Piggybacking on their energy and insights could help you regain inspiration.

Offer your assistance. To gain purpose, you might provide coaching or mentorship to a younger employee, volunteer to pick up slack for a member of your team who's struggling, or offer support to a colleague in a different division. You could also look for opportunities outside your day job at a local community service-based organization.

Craft your current job with an eye toward purpose. Job shaping is another strategy that can spark our dormant enthusiasm for work. Look for ways to make new contributions in your job so that your presence at your organization feels more meaningful. Think about how your strengths, skills, and passions could help your organization deal with the current moment's crisis-related challenges.

Seek out and be grateful for colleagues. Finally, expressing gratitude grounds you and provides a counterbalance to the negativity that crisis and uncertainty generate. Put simply, telling others what they mean to you is a meaningful experience in its own right. "Those moments of connection—taking a minute and saying, 'I appreciate you and I really enjoy working with you'—are powerful," the authors write.[61]

Ideally, the work we do daily is beneficial to something we value. For example, a chef who values healthy social connections might focus on the way food helps others to create social connections in her restaurant. That makes her cooking more than just a way to earn a living. A mother who loves learning might focus on reading with her young children who are just starting school. It's a way of helping them to enjoy what she values: education. A business partner who values teamwork might look for ways to include additional employees in a project, and ensure they receive recognition for their work.

Let's go back one last time to the tennis analogy. When life serves up a particular emotion, does running after it make your life better or worse? Ironically by accepting it, even for a millisecond you are more able to let it go. But if it makes your life better, if it's giving you important clues, if it turns you toward things that you value, then go after it and delve deeper to discover - what is significant to me here. You'll be amazed how much better you feel when your emotions, efforts, and values all align.

FEEL BETTER WITH THESE RESOURCES

Want all of the book exercises in one spot? Download your Better workbook.

https://drshahana.com/workbook

....

Want more? Follow me on my journey to build emotional clarity and capacity here:

My website is: www.drshahana.com

https://www.youtube.com/@dr.shahana-feelbetter

www.linkedin.com/in/shahana-alibhai-feelbetter

https://www.instagram.com/@thedrshahana

CHAPTER 7

ACT

REFRAME AND CHANGE THE EMOTIONS THAT AFFECT YOU THE MOST.

When I was a child, I loved visiting my grandmother's house. Every room featured its own unique treasures: in the kitchen, for example, a candy jar perched on a shelf, filled to the brim with homemade toffees. On a table in the living room, an old cookie tin sat like a treasure chest, hoarding handfuls of coins from around the world. Discovery and wonder abounded in every room, even the bathroom. That's where I read the little clipping my grandmother had carefully cut and taped to the mirror. It extolled the benefits of drinking eight glasses of water a day.

When I read that healthy advice, the six-year-old me decided to act immediately. I did as the clipping advised, with one slight misapplication. Rather than drinking water throughout the day, I thought I was supposed to drink eight glasses of water all at once. I was chugging glass number six when I realized I didn't feel so good.

EMOTIONS AREN'T ALL-OR-NOTHING

Many of us practice this all-or-nothing mode of thinking when it comes to our emotions. We either assume we have to do every-thing—go to yoga, meditate, analyze what we're feeling, discuss it with others, and journal our way to enlightenment—or we decide we're going to abandon ourselves to apathy, suppressing our way into emotional oblivion.

This chapter is focused on actions: reasonable actions. In previ-ous chapters you have learned about the power of perception. By now, hopefully, you have bolstered yourself with some semblance of self-awareness. You have witnessed that behind your greatest emotions lie your deepest values. Now it's time to figure out what to do with what you've learned. Let's look at how to move from meaningful understanding to meaningful action.

When dealing with emotions, you don't have to do the equiv-alent of drinking glass after glass of water until you're ready to burst. Working through your emotions on the way to feeling better can instead be a pleasant relief, like sipping cool water when you feel thirsty. Let's look at some ways that, as you become more self-aware, you can utilize your perceptions to your advantage.

THE STRESS RESPONSE CYCLE

Here are three important principles concerning emotions:

- *Emotions have a beginning, middle, and end.*
- *You decide whether you will* stay *with the emotion or* shift *toward something else.*
- *Shifting requires you to complete the three stages of the stress response cycle: the alarm/reaction stage, the resistance stage, and the exhaustion stage.*

In their book *Burnout: The Secret to Unlocking the Stress Cycle*, Emily and Amelia Nagoski conclude that our stress response is adapted to the environment in which we live. An age-old example of this is being chased by a lion, which causes human adrenal glands to release a flood of hormones that cause the heart to beat faster, pulsing more blood and oxygen into the legs so we can flee. This is a great example of the sympathetic nervous system activating the body's "fight-or-flight" response.

"There [are] only two possible outcomes," Emily says. "Either you get eaten by the lion—in which case, none of the rest of this matters—or you manage to make it all the way back to your village. And somebody sees you running and opens the door and waves you in. And you both stand with your shoulder against the door until the lion finally gives up. And when that happens, you look at the person who just saved your life, and you are flooded with this sense of gratitude, connection, and peace. And that's biochemically the complete stress response cycle."[62]

Safe from the lion, your body would then respond to the parasympathetic nervous system, which relaxes your body after periods of stress or danger and helps to run life-sustaining processes, like digestion, when you feel safe. You would feel your heart rate coming down, your breathing return to normal, and your tight muscles gradually loosening.

In our daily lives, however, few of us are chased by four-legged carnivores. "Our stressors tend to be things that are not actually going to threaten our lives," Emily continues. "The jerk at work, traffic, these things are not going to kill us, but they do elevate our stress response in a similar way, but they don't offer us the same opportunity to complete the stress response cycle. So we're walking around with a couple decades of incomplete activated stress response cycles..."[63]

Our stressors are more like the never-ending paper cuts of life, and some sting more than others. When such stressors are resolved, traffic flows smoothly: the work project is handed in, or you found the 15 library books your child swore they never had. But that doesn't mean the stress response is over.

This is a key point. Just because the stressor might be resolved doesn't mean we're finished dealing with it. We still need to complete the stress response cycle.

WHEN STRESS IS CONSTANT

Health writer Zia Sherrell, in a post reviewed by medical advisor Debra Rose Wilson, discusses the three stages of the cycle. "Stress isn't just an emotion," Sherrell says. "When you experience an external stressor, it triggers a series of complex reactions in the body. ... The cycle is natural and happens automatically. It should only last for a short period before you recover and continue with business as usual. But, when stress is constant—or you never give yourself time to recover—the cycle can persist and continue indefinitely."[64]

JUST BECAUSE THE STRESSOR MIGHT BE RESOLVED DOESN'T MEAN WE'RE FINISHED DEALING WITH IT. WE STILL NEED TO COMPLETE THE STRESS RESPONSE CYCLE.

The alarm stage, she says, "tells your body how to react ... Basically, you're ready to run or rumble!" Then, during the resistance stage, the body begins to recover, but "it remains in a state of heightened alert and stress hormones remain high." Coping with the continuing stress "can lead to poor sleep, poor concentration, and irritability." If you don't complete the stress cycle, she warns, then the body repeats the stress response, which can lead to chronic stress.

She recommends getting enough sleep, avoiding taking on too much—both at home and at work, using physical touch to create comfort, finding healthy ways to release emotions such as "talking to a friend, writing in a journal, or venting to a therapist," breathing deeply, and seeking professional health care when you feel constantly stressed.

Completing the stress response cycle takes time and effort, Sherrell says. "But it's worth it to feel calmer and more in control of your health and well-being."[65]

LIKE RIPPLES ON THE WATER

Imagine throwing rocks in a lake. As a rock hits the surface of the water, what happens? You see a beautiful ripple. The stress response is like this expanding circle, with a beginning, middle, and end.

The problem is that most of us get stuck in the middle. Remember, most of the time we cannot control the stressor (the "what" we discussed in Chapter 3.) The "how," also discussed in Chapter 3, is our ability to move through the stress response. And this is in our direct control.

So, what happens if we don't move all the way through the stress response cycle? It's like having the ripple pass over us not once, but over and over again. It can lead to years and years of allowing ourselves to live with chronic stress, whether or not the stressor is still there. Chronic stress creates a cascade of mechanical, chemical, and maladaptive processing that can influence multiple organ systems—cardiovascular, digestive, or even reproductive.

THE POWER OF ACCEPTING EMOTIONS

In order to move through the emotional cycle, you need to accept that you have the emotion in the first place. Sounds easy right? Just the opposite. I didn't even know I was doing this until I saw patients do the same thing: completely and utterly refuse to believe that they could be capable of having such an emotion. Guilt? Never! Envy? Of course not. Disappointment? I'm too strong for that. We have these types of internal dialogue because we assume that by having a certain emotion we are somehow "less than" or "not strong enough." The only way to truly move through the emotional cycle is by accepting it—I say even for a "nanosecond," but you still have to accept it.

Life coach Shmuel Brody says when we experience uncomfortable feelings like fear, anxiety, or guilt we often attempt to alleviate them by explaining to ourselves why it doesn't make sense to feel it. We consider a string of reasons to do away with that feeling forever. "Moreover, attempting to explain our fears away is an act of non-acceptance. We are uncomfortable having a feeling and wish to do away with it"[66]

Then, when the feeling passes, we believe we are mentally ready to thrive from then on, but of course we aren't. That's because our feelings cannot be reasoned with through logic. Feelings are messages the brain sends based not only upon the current stimuli but also by what's happened in the past. They are not rationally induced and will not go away with rationalizations.

MOVING THROUGH THE CYCLE

Then how do we move completely through the stress response cycle? Close your eyes and imagine a recent time when you had a strong, perhaps uncomfortable, emotion. One occurred for me recently during a business meeting. What initially had sounded like a favorable partnership was now, according to me, being misconstrued into an agreement where I felt like the less-productive piece of the team. The meeting left my head spinning and my mind trying to separate fact from fiction.

How should I respond?

Remember: every emotion gives you three clues. Imagine 3 rocks piled neatly upon each other like an inukshuk. Each of these rocks stands for a clue that an emotion gives you.

These are:

- Sensation
- Story
- Significance

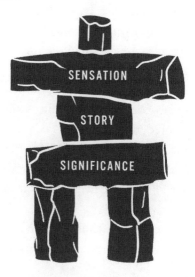

146

HERE IS A BRIEF REFRESHER:

Sensation

"A sensation is triggered by the experiencer's environment and gives rise to a perception, which corresponds to the way individuals process the stimuli they receive," says a journal article published by Stephanie Beligon et al. "…Sensation and emotion involve the experiencer's body and seem to serve the same end, i.e., the individual's survival and adaptation to his/her environment."[67]

Since sensations lead to perceptions, it may be helpful to be aware of the specific sensations that lead to specific perceptions. Does a certain sensation always lead you to a certain perception? How accurate is that perception? By noticing these patterns, it may become easier to spot problems before they become overwhelming.

Story

We've talked about the internal narrator and the story you tell yourself based on emotions and experiences, especially early experiences with those you consider experts. But as you are moving toward action, here are a few things to keep in mind. (See Chapter Four for additional detail.)

- Remember that self-compassion encompasses three main parts: kindness, mindfulness, and connection with others, rather than a judgmental comparison to them.
- Trying to witness and reflect on your own internal story can be like asking your toddler to clean your beloved crystal vase—it can leave you in a state of anxiety until the task is complete.
- Identifying your inner narrator is one thing; being willing to listen in a kind, non-judgmental manner is something

SELF-COMPASSION ENCOMPASSES THREE MAIN PARTS: KINDNESS, MINDFULNESS, AND CONNECTION WITH OTHERS, RATHER THAN A JUDGMENTAL COMPARISON TO THEM.

else. This requires practice and patience. It is likely one of the hardest parts of self-compassion.

• An easier entry point to self-compassion is connecting to others in a similar situation. For example, don't say to yourself, "This person has it harder or easier than I do," or, "This only happens to me." Rather, allow yourself to realize that others are likely in a similar situation.

Significance

The forces we feel in life are like a magnet; we are attracted to our values and repelled by our fears. What you value shines a light on what you fear as well. For example, valuing connection might be rooted in a fear of being alone; valuing honesty might be rooted in a fear that someone will take advantage of you. Understanding what you value and how that value triggers emotions gives significance to your self-awareness. That awareness becomes significant when it helps you move from reacting to emotions to seeing them for what they are and shifting from negative to positive responses.

MOVING THROUGH THE STRESS RESPONSE CYCLE, ONE "S" AT A TIME

Take out your mental highlighter and remember these three "S" words. Most of the time when we talk about "completing the cycle" we focus on the sensation. Just like being chased by a lion as in example above, the spotlight here was on your heart racing and your fast breathing. What will be presented to you below is the "BETS" acronym: a simple, easy-to-remember set of tools that can be used to move through the "sensation" component of the emotion you are feeling. However, to fully understand your emotions, I recommend that the two other "S" words be addressed. Luckily we spent a lot of time discussing the "story in your head" in Chapter 5 as well as our value systems in Chapter 6.

Let's go back to my example of the meeting:

- *Sensation:* After the meeting my chest felt heavy. My shoulders started reaching up toward my ears. I felt jittery and tense at the same time.
- *Story.* What *was* the story I was telling myself in my head? I tried not to judge my narrative as right or wrong. I tried not to be the hero or victim. I just observed the story. In my case, my inner narrator was telling me, "This person thinks less of me. They think I'm not pulling my weight. They want to stop working with me." We have to be aware of the story we are spinning.
- *Significance.* I really value productivity. Moreover, I have a deep sense of wanting to be liked (who doesn't?!). Therefore, during this meeting when it felt like the tone changed from collaboration to interrogation, I immediately felt I wasn't needed anymore on the team.

After completing those steps, you are now in the driver's seat. I still felt dejected and upset; of course, the event had just happened. However, after going through the three "Ss" I was better able to understand *why*. Remember, you cannot change an emotion by wishing it away. What you can do, however, is soften the emotion by understanding it.

LIKE SOFTENED BUTTER

As a little girl I loved to bake. Once I discovered the power of the 30-year-old hand mixer in my mom's kitchen, nothing could hold me back. Creaming the butter, sugar, and eggs together was always my favorite step, adding a little vanilla to the mix as well. When you mix those ingredients together, they create a perfect shade of yellow. But I learned through a sad experience that cold, hard butter is a problem. It's best to leave the butter out at room temperature so that it can soften before you go at it with an electric hand mixer. Then, rather than dealing with stiff lumps of fat, room temperature butter becomes aerated, with the promise of a fluffy cake to follow.

The process of softening butter and the process of shifting emotions have a lot in common. Setting butter out to soften is a small act: subtle and smooth. Shifting emotions can be the same—a gradual softening that is subtle and smooth. Sometimes the best way to change an emotion is to soften it through working through the three "Ss": sensation, story and significance.

SOMETIMES THE BEST WAY TO CHANGE AN EMOTION IS TO SOFTEN IT.

For most of us, the best entry point into this is starting with the sensation in your body because this can be the most noticeable and possibly most bothersome as well. The BETS acronym allows you to soften the sensation of the emotion. After doing one, or two—or even all—of these tools, you hopefully will have created a bit of space between you and the emotion so that you can move on to the other two Ss: undercovering the story in your head and where your emotional compass is pointing (i.e., significance).

The BETS acronym is one of my favorite tools to work through hard emotions. I've developed it to both soften the emotion and move through the physiological aspects of the stress response cycle. BETS stands for:

- B: breathing.
- E: exercise and environment.
- T: touch, temperature, and time out.
- S: social connection

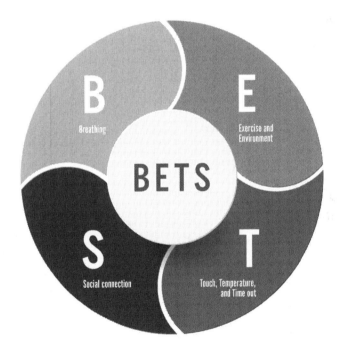

Let's look at each of these stress-softeners individually.

Breathing

Two of my favorite breathing exercises are:

1. *The Physiological Sigh.* Also known as cyclical sighing, this technique developed by Stanford University professor and neuroscientist Andrew D. Huberman can "instantly turn off that panicky feeling of mounting stress we all dread." Here's how it works:
   - Sit or stand. Exhale fully through the mouth, breathing all your air out.
   - Using your diaphragm, inhale through your nose until your lungs feel completely full.
   - Holding that same breath, use your nose to take in one final sharp inhale to draw even more air into your lungs.
   - Exhale slowly through the mouth, breathing all the air out. If you want to calm down quickly, make your exhales longer than your inhales.
   - Repeat this cycle two-to-three times.

2. *4-7-8 Breathing.* This breathing exercise, developed by Dr. Andrew Weil, M.D., is based on an ancient yoga technique called *pranayama*. It is designed to help bring the body back into balance by forcing the body and mind to regulate breathing, rather than replaying worries and concerns. Start by resting the tip of your tongue against the roof of your mouth, right behind your top front teeth. You'll need to keep your tongue in place throughout the exercise. Then follow these steps, in the cycle of one breath:
   - Part your lips. Exhale completely through your mouth while making a whooshing sound.

- Close your lips. Inhale through your nose as you count to four in your head.
- Then, hold your breath for seven seconds.
- Exhale from your mouth for eight seconds, making a whooshing sound again.

Repeat this pattern for four full breaths. The seven seconds spent holding your breath is the most critical part of this exercise. Practice 4-7-8 breathing for four breaths when you're first starting out. Then gradually work up to eight full breaths.

"Once you develop this breathing technique by practicing it every day, twice a day, it will be a very useful tool that you will always have with you," Dr. Weil says. "Use it whenever anything upsetting happens—before you react." [68]

Breathing is a necessary part of life. It may seem like a simple thing compared to sometimes complex emotional challenges. But the statement, "Take a breath and calm down," is great advice when stress runs amok, whether you use breathing techniques or simply need a time out.

EXERCISE AND ENVIRONMENT

Getting moving and changing your environment are two proven antidotes for stress.

First, let's address the need for physical exercise. "People can use exercise to stifle the buildup of stress in several ways," says an article from Harvard Medical School. "Exercise, such as taking a brisk walk shortly after feeling stressed, not only deepens breathing but also helps relieve muscle tension. Movement therapies such as yoga, tai chi, and qi gong combine fluid movements with deep breathing and mental focus, all of which can induce calm." [69]

Sometimes a short stroll can help you unwind. Other times, you might want to consider a punching bag!

"To help stress, you do not need much exercise," says Bradley Bogdan of the Department of Psychiatry in the Texas A&M College of Medicine.[70] "What matters the most is that you do it regularly, more so than strenuously." Set a goal to move your body for 20–60 minutes each day—biking, dancing, running, gardening, jumping rope, etc.

Changing your environment can also help when stress is building. "Visiting greenspaces and being exposed to natural environments can reduce stress," Bogdan says. "Natural-looking spaces have a big effect on minimizing stress and improving your overall health. Simply viewing representations of nature helps reduce stress. If you are feeling chronically stressed, try to incorporate more nature-themed elements into your work and living space."[71]

Stress relief may be a trip to the park, a drive up the canyon, or watching the sunset at the beach.

TOUCH, TEMPERATURE, AND TIME OUT

Our physical senses—such as sight, touch, smell, taste, and hearing—can also help alleviate stress. Think, for example, of how listening to certain music can relax you, make you want to dance, or cause you to happily sing along. Here are a few additional examples of how physical senses can help you feel better.

Touch: This sense can offer reassurance and comfort. Some examples of stress reduction methods that incorporate touch:

- *The Butterfly Hug* was developed to help hurricane survivors and is often used in treating post-traumatic stress disorder (PTSD). But it can also be used in everyday situations to calm down, get grounded, and focus on the present moment. It involves crossing your hands over your chest and interlocking your thumbs, then tapping your hands like butterfly wings as you observe your emotions—just observing as if you were watching clouds passing by.[72]

- *The Six-Second Kiss*, popularized by clinical psychologist Dr. John Gottman, is intended to bring couples closer together by replacing a quick peck on the lips with a kiss that's slightly longer. "It stops the busyness in your brain and puts your focus on your partner at that moment," says certified therapist Kari Rusnak. "Kissing can be a good exercise in mindfulness."[73]

- *The 20-Second Hug* can decrease stress levels, increase oxytocin (a "love hormone" that promotes positive feelings), and facilitate bonding between partners, according to Tracy P. Alloway, PhD. "It works in a beautiful, positive circular fashion: When you give love, you receive love, which makes you want to keep giving love. And it works the same for men and women."[74]

Temperature: Alternating between hot and cold is often used as a means of dealing with physical pain. Hot/cold therapy, such as hot/cold showers, can be used as a method of adjusting hormone levels. Scandinavians have long advocated the benefits of running from a heated sauna to plunge into icy water nearby. Cold water swimming has become increasingly trendy, and Wim Hof, a Dutchman whose method combines enduring extreme

cold with breathing techniques, has attracted millions of online followers.

The *New York Times* reports that "those who swear by the benefits of cold water say it leaves them feeling invigorated, clear headed, and better able to handle stress. Some say that it has helped them cope with grief, anxiety, depression, and other mental health challenges."[75]

"What if the key to managing your stress is … more stress?" asks the *Wall Street Journal*, noting that "a growing body of biological research … indicates that short intermittent bouts of stress such as heat, exercise, and dietary restriction can strengthen your ability to withstand chronic stress."[76]

Elissa Epsel, PhD., a professor in the psychiatry department at the University of California, San Francisco, says such practices "create short-term spikes of biological stress followed by recovery, ease and deep restoration and that is otherwise hard to get."[77]

Time Out: How often have you said to a child who's out of control, "You need a time out"? But do you ever say it to yourself? Truth be told, we all need a time out now and then, especially when we feel things are spinning out of control.

"Time-outs provide relief from a downward spiral of an increasingly agitated or hostile interaction by providing a cooling off period in which both parties can gain their composure and eventually re-engage when calmer heads can prevail," Linda and Charlie Bloom say in an article in *Psychology Today*.[78]

Based on their experience in counseling couples, they add this caution: "There must be an intention on the part of each partner to use the time to settle themselves down, defuse their emotions, in a way that enables them to come back together bringing more openness to hear the other person without reacting with judgment, blame, or defensiveness. This level of vulnerability is almost impossible to achieve when we're in the grip of intense emotions and feeling threatened by our partner. For this reason, it's necessary for both partners to do whatever they need to do in order to adjust their attitude in a way that will increase the chances of having a productive interaction after the reunion."[79]

DIGITAL TIME OUT

We think of our phone as the ultimate distraction and for some, this certainly might be the case. Unfortunately, our cellular devices aren't going anywhere, so it's time to start using them to our advantage. This is why I came up with my version of "digital time out." With three active boys, life is often unpredictable, chaotic, and extremely loud at the best of times. I often find myself escaping to my bathroom even for a moment of quiet (although a lock on the door would make this much more beneficial). One of the reasons we get swept away on our phones is that we don't even know what we are doing half the time. We bounce from social media to social media site, online shopping, Amazon purchases, getting updated on the news, and everything in between. For someone trying to get "peace and quiet," our impulsive browser history certainly doesn't reflect this.

The first thing I do is set a time limit: How much time am I going to be on my phone? In my case, it's usually three-to-five minutes before someone finds me hidden away. The second thing is determining an outcome: How do I want to feel afterwards? Do I want to connect with a friend with a quick text? Do I want to laugh? Do I want to accomplish a quick task that would take less than 60 seconds to do? Set an objective, and even better, figure out how you want to feel when it's over. After these two easy steps, the floor is yours: remove the guilt and stigma and bask in the bliss of the "digital time out."

"It's important to accept that … we're probably going to need to carry a phone," Strohmeyer says, but notes, "You can choose your actions rather than blaming the world for these interruptions. Because that's what these devices are set up to do, to interrupt the heck out of you." She recommends taking a deep breath and relaxing before answering the phone. You can also turn off automatic alerts, unsubscribe from unwanted email lists, and avoid controversial websites.

SOCIAL CONNECTION

"Humans are wired to connect, and this connection affects our health," says an article in the *American Journal of Lifestyle Medicine*. "From psychological theories to recent research, there is significant evidence that social support and feeling connected can help people maintain a healthy body mass index, control blood sugars, improve cancer survival, decrease cardiovascular mortality, decrease depressive symptoms, mitigate posttraumatic stress disorder symptoms, and improve overall mental health. Individuals need connections in their lives in the workplace and at home. Fostering these connections is critical to health and wellness."[80]

According to a post from the Harvard Medical School, confidants, friends, acquaintances, co-workers, relatives, spouses, and companions all provide a life-enhancing social net—and may increase longevity. "It's not clear why, but the buffering theory holds that people who enjoy close relationships with family and friends receive emotional support that indirectly helps to sustain them at times of chronic stress and crisis."[81]

Psychiatrist Edward Hallowell, M.D., in his landmark book, *Connect*, notes that, "A five-minute conversation can make all the difference in the world if the parties participate actively. To make it work, you have to set aside what you're doing, put down the memo you were reading, disengage from your laptop, abandon your daydream and bring your attention to bear upon the person you are with. Usually, when you do this, the other person (or people) will feel the energy and respond in kind, naturally."[82]

Another benefit of social connections is that they provide opportunities for us to laugh with other people. "Laughter is part of a universal language of basic emotions that all humans recognize," according to studies at Wayne State University. [83]

"Laughter is a unique communication medium, common to all human societies speaking different languages," says J. J. M. Askenasy of the Department of Neurology at the Tel Aviv School of Medicine in Israel. "Laughter has a mood elevating and relaxing effect."[84]

It is said that children laugh up to 400 times a day; we as adults, only a paltry 14 times a day. Just a few minutes of laughter each day may improve your health in more ways than you realize. Laughter causes the release of endorphins that increase the body's painkilling response. This can fight chronic pain, improve your mood, and lower stress. Laughter also reduces production of stress hormones like cortisol and may activate cells to fight off infection. Laughter causes you to breathe more deeply, sending additional oxygen throughout your body, which promotes healthy cell growth. It can also reduce tension and make you

IT IS SAID THAT CHILDREN LAUGH UP TO 400 TIMES A DAY; WE AS ADULTS, ONLY A PALTRY 14 TIMES A DAY.

feel calmer. Joking about a problem rather than ruminating on it may also help reduce stress.

In some circumstances, laughter may in fact be the best medicine—or at least a potent one.

RUBBER OR GLASS?

Shifting by using elements found in the BETS acronym can be a helpful way to move through the stress cycle. Hopefully, you've found some useful tactics and tricks here to deal with tough emotions, shifting from detrimental emotions or thoughts to those that are more positive.

When we decide to act, we work to reframe emotions that are affecting us the most. As I counsel with people, I ask them to consider: "Are you rubber or are you glass?" In other words, when you have a situation that causes you to feel uncomfortable emotions, do you shatter or are you resilient? If you find yourself being shattered by tough emotions, employing some of these techniques can help you build resilience and strengthen your ability to bounce back.

Remember, there are hundreds of ways to respond to stress. The point is to find a few you can turn to in times of need.

CHAPTER 8

TALK

COMMUNICATE YOUR EMOTIONS AND ASK FOR HELP.

I wasn't exactly popular in high school. Well, I *was* popular with the science, math, and English teachers. But I hardly think that counted with the other kids.

A few days before graduation, a classmate who I thought was my friend approached me. She told me sheepishly that the only reason she had been hanging out with me was so that she could cheat off my papers and assignments. She admitted she had been copying off me for an entire year. That happened several decades ago, and it still stings.

I learned early on in my schooling that academics represented safety to me. I was good at studying. I didn't mind working hard.

And somehow being at the top of my class in every academic discipline seemed like a good alternative to being popular socially, or even to having close friends. It took me a long time after that to learn to trust other people and believe that they valued me as a person, and not just for my brain or what I could do for them. I'm not alone in this feeling of isolation. Many people have similar concerns about connecting with others. And yet, we all need to connect.

POSITIVE CONNECTIVITY

In Chapter 7, we discussed the importance of moving from meaningful understanding to meaningful action. Now it's time to understand how positive connections with others can help us to build and maintain meaningful momentum as we continue along the path of feeling better.

In this chapter we will explore the concept of connectivity, because feeling better doesn't exist solely in our heads or hearts. We often feel better because of our connections to other people. And when we communicate our emotions to others, we can learn from their responses and observations. What's more, we can ask for help when we need it. In this chapter, we will explore the power of connection, the foundation of true connection, the right time for connection, and the way to enhance connection by listening with two ears instead of one.

THE POWER OF CONNECTION

When I was growing up, my favorite TV show was *I Love Lucy*. In fact, it's still my all-time favorite. Lucille Ball is said to have shared this secret for staying young: "Live honestly, eat slowly, and lie about your age."

Although that's a funny statement, research offers a more honest assessment of how to stay young. In what has been called the most extensive study of long life ever conducted, eight decades of research involving 1,500 Californians show that many long-held beliefs about aging are far from true. For example:

- People don't die from working long hours at a challenging job; many who worked the hardest lived the longest.
- Getting married doesn't necessarily mean you will live longer.
- Worrying is not necessarily bad for your health.
- Vigorous forms of exercise will not always help you live longer than gardening and walking.

The Longevity Project, a book by health scientists Dr. Howard S. Friedman and Dr. Leslie R. Martin, reveals that what matters in the long run are things like personality traits, relationships, experiences, and career paths that naturally keep you vital. They make this key point: "Social connection should be the first place to look for improving health and longevity."[85]

So, what exactly is social connection? The Centers for Disease Control and Prevention (CDCP) call it social connectedness, defined as "the degree to which people have and perceive a desired number, quality, and diversity of relationships that create a sense of belonging, and being cared for, valued, and supported." Social connections, the CDCP says, generate stable and supportive relationships; they foster healthy choices; promote better mental and physical health outcomes; and enable people to cope with stress, anxiety, depression, and personal difficulties.[86]

Healthy connections provide the opportunity for regular, meaningful social exchanges; a sense of support from family, friends, and community; a sense of belonging and having close bonds with others; access to safe gathering places; and having more than one person to turn to for emotional and physical support.

Friedman and Martin also found that those who had a larger social network *and* felt that they were helping others (such as advising and caring for them) were more likely to live a longer life. Those who felt they had someone to call on in time of need and those who felt loved or cared for reported feeling better, even though they did not necessarily reap the same benefit of longevity.[87]

MAKE YOUR SECONDS COUNT

It's easy to think that maintaining social connections requires too much time and effort, especially as adults (who own cable TV and the Internet). It becomes another item on our never-ending checklist of things we ought to do.

"In today's age, we live busy lives, trying to strike a balance between work, school, hobbies, self-care, and more," says the Canadian Mental Health Association (CMHA). "Often, our social connections fall by the wayside. But connecting with others is more important than you might think. Social connection can lower anxiety and depression, help us regulate our emotions, lead to higher self-esteem and empathy, and actually improve our immune systems. By neglecting our need to connect, we put our health at risk."[88]

But what if I told you that you can derive proven health benefits in a matter of seconds from the social connections you already have? In Chapter 7 we described the six-second kiss and the 20-second hug. As their names suggest, both involve a minimal amount of time, either kissing your partner for six seconds or hugging someone you love for 20 seconds. The time duration of each of these are mindfully chosen to allow you to sink deeper into the moment. Physiologically, this allows the release of chemicals such as oxytocin, serotonin, and dopamine, cultivating the feeling of connection and togetherness.

Now let's add one additional short-duration social connection enhancer. I call it the 60-second phone call.

I coined the name after I found I was hesitant to call friends and was just texting them instead. In fact, these days calling others can feel like the equivalent of showing up at someone's house and ringing their doorbell. How rude! It wasn't until a good friend of mine started calling me regularly just to say, "Hi!" that I realized a short phone call can do a lot of good and wasn't intrusive at all. My friend's conversations were always short—anywhere from 20 seconds to 60 seconds—and showed me that by making just a little bit more effort, rather than simply texting, I could really connect. I could hear this friend's voice and have an actual, though brief, conversation.

Too often we assume that the other person might be busy, that we might be interrupting, or that the conversation will be too short to say anything significant. But here are some realities: If they are busy, they won't answer. And perhaps they would actually welcome a short interruption from a friend. A conversation can be concise and still be meaningful.

"The reality is that we're living in a time of true disconnection," CMHA says. "While technology seems to connect us more than ever, the screens around us disconnect us from nature, from ourselves, and from others. Wi-Fi alone isn't enough to fulfill our social needs—we need face-to-face interaction to thrive. Technology should be enhancing our connection to others, not replacing it."[89]

BUILDING A FOUNDATION FOR TRUE CONNECTION

One of the most common ways to build connection is through conversations. After all, that's how we get acquainted and share experiences. But how often do we fail to build connections because we focus the conversation on ourselves rather than on the person we're talking with?

For example, imagine you're at a swanky social gathering, talking to someone you just met. You find yourself trying to think of a witty response, something clever to say that will put you in a good light. We have all done that, rather than doing the one thing we *should* be doing instead: truly listening. I find myself especially prone to this behavior when I feel uncomfortable, find it hard to follow the drift of a conversation, or for some reason feel the need to pretend I am someone I'm really not.

Little did I know a name exists for this. It's called shift response versus support response. After studying hundreds of informal dinner conversations, sociologist Charles Derber of Boston College found that responses given during conversations typically fall into two categories: shift or support.[90] Here are some examples:

Shift Response
Colleague: I went on an amazing hike yesterday.

You: I hiked for miles two days ago and my calves are still feeling it.

Support Response
Colleague: I went on an amazing hike yesterday.

You: Oh, cool! Where was it? What was the view like?

See the difference?

The shift response, which is the more common response, means you shift attention away from the speaker to yourself. Just like moving a spotlight on a dark stage, a shift response moves the light from the other person to you. A shift response steers the conversation in a way that may help you feel like you're gaining control. But it may also make the other person feel like you're not really concerned about them. Derber referred to this shift response as "conversational narcissism."[91]

> THE SHIFT RESPONSE, WHICH IS THE MORE COMMON RESPONSE, MEANS YOU SHIFT ATTENTION AWAY FROM THE SPEAKER TO YOURSELF.

In contrast, the support response shines the spotlight on the speaker, asking them to elaborate or enhance the information they have already given. It demonstrates genuine interest and curiosity in them and their experiences, a willingness to learn from them. The question then becomes, why do we (and I'm including myself) engage in the shift response more than the support response?

Journalist and author Celeste Headlee offers this technical explanation: "The insula, an area of the brain deep inside the cerebral cortex, takes in the information that people tell us and then tries to find a relevant experience in our memory banks that can give context to the information. It's mostly helpful: the brain is trying to make sense of what we hear and see. Subconsciously, we find similar experiences and add them to what's happening at the moment, and then the whole package of information is sent to the limbic regions, the part of the brain just below the cerebrum. That's where some trouble can arise—instead of helping us better understand someone else's experience, our own experiences can

THE SUPPORT RESPONSE SHINES THE SPOTLIGHT ON THE SPEAKER, ASKING THEM TO ELABORATE OR ENHANCE THE INFORMATION THEY HAVE ALREADY GIVEN.

distort our perceptions of what the other person is saying or experiencing."[92]

A study published in the *Journal of Neuroscience* concluded that, "When assessing the world around us and our fellow humans, we use ourselves as a yardstick and tend to project our own emotional state onto others."[93] Our feelings can distort our capacity for empathy, and although this "emotionally driven egocentricity" is normally recognized and corrected by the brain, sometimes, especially when we're making quick decisions, our empathy may be severely limited.

I believe one of the main reasons we engage in the shift response is because we all crave a feeling of competence, credibility, and acceptance. By constantly shifting the spotlight back to ourselves, we are endeavoring to convince others of our own merits and values.

"For social beings who crave love and belonging, wanting to be liked and caring about the effect we have on others is healthy and allows us to make connections," says psychotherapist Allison Abrams. "However, where we get into trouble is when our self-worth is contingent upon whether we win someone's approval or not."[94]

So, here are some additional questions you need to ask yourself:

- When you seek engagement with others, what is your goal? Is it to find acceptance or is it to foster connection?

- How do *you* feel when you're talking with someone who always steers the conversation back to *their* needs and desires? Does that make you want to connect with them, or does it make you feel they care more about themselves than they do about others?

Now, it's not lost on me that acceptance and connection are related in a chicken-and-egg kind of way. Which comes first? The more connected you feel with like-minded and supportive individuals, does that translate into more self-acceptance? And is the opposite equally true, that the more accepting you are of yourself the more authentic you are? And doesn't authenticity, in turn, create robust connections?

To build a foundation for true connection, you must cultivate a desire to learn about others, to be curious about them, to care about establishing *their* competence, credibility, and acceptance. As you connect meaningfully with others, you'll find self-acceptance is a healthy byproduct.

THE RIGHT TIME FOR CONNECTION

One day my three-year-old son came home from daycare with a list created by the staff (with his help) of two categories: things he loved and things he disliked. Top on the love list were candy (no surprise) and his favorite animated series, Paw Patrol. The dislike list included broccoli (no surprise), sharing his toys (he is three after all), and monsters. What was weird to me was that he mentioned monsters, because before this list he had never spoken about them. And when I asked him to tell me more about monsters, he couldn't tell me anything—not what they looked like, what color they were,

ONE OF THE MAIN REASONS WE
ENGAGE IN THE SHIFT RESPONSE
IS BECAUSE WE ALL CRAVE
A FEELING OF COMPETENCE,
CREDIBILITY, AND ACCEPTANCE.

why he was scared of them, nothing. The one thing he *could* tell me for sure was that monsters only came out in the dark.

Anxiety can be considered a monster. It breeds in the dark, not in a "lights out" kind of way, but in the secretive black hole it creates around itself.

Years ago, after my son was born, my colleagues planned a baby shower. It was supposed to be a joyous, happy occasion featuring food, gifts, and games. Everyone seemed excited about it, except for me. Here we were, in a workplace that dealt almost exclusively with mental health, and I couldn't bring myself to tell them that I was going through postpartum anxiety. Rather than sharing what I was experiencing, I kept telling them I was too tired or too busy to party; and asked my work friends over and over to postpone the shower.

When I stood on a TEDx stage in 2019, one of the first things I did was to say the words, "postpartum anxiety." I remember feeling utterly sick at confessing to the world that this was part of my life, that somehow people would judge me and think I was weak. The ironic part was that I didn't even share my full truth, that not only did I have postpartum obsessive-compulsive disorder (OCD), but that I have had pure obsessional OCD since I was four-or-five years old. I had spent decades of my life feeling like something was totally and completely broken in me and not knowing where or how to fix it.

It was on a podcast several years later that I decided to use correct terminology. I told the host about my postpartum OCD, and the host responded with questions I found difficult to answer:

- "What exactly is postpartum OCD?"
- "What kinds of thoughts do women with postpartum OCD have?"
- "What is the treatment for postpartum OCD?"

The fact is, none of the answers to these questions are simple. But I felt that offering responses was important. After that, every podcast I went on, if asked, I told my truth. I spoke honestly about my symptoms, and about the fear, shame, and isolation they generated. And as I spoke about it more often, I found that eventually I could say the words "postpartum OCD" with less repulsion. I also found that by sharing my experience, I gained the ability to understand that I was not alone in dealing with it. Others enduring the same struggle came forward to share what they had gone through or were going through; those who had not experienced what I had still offered sympathy, compassion, and support. Most importantly, I acknowledged myself to myself.

In Chapter 4 we said that the pathway to feeling better begins with acknowledgement, crosses a bridge called self-awareness, and leads to self-compassion. An integral part of this pathway is authenticity. For me, sharing my story became a vital part of being authentic. Notice that I'm saying *for me*. Your story, your journey, might be different. However, if you feel that sharing your experience is something you want to try, here are some tips that might be helpful.

- *Choose your audience.* One of the first times I ever shared my true story, it was with an acquaintance. This acquaintance was someone I knew professionally, someone I inherently trusted, but someone I was not close with by any means. That may have been fortunate. Research suggests that this may be a healthy way to begin sharing something that is difficult for you to share. Harvard sociologist Mario Luis Small found that, "At times the best confidant is one with some distance." He added that, "Approaching individuals they are not especially close to appears to be what adult Americans do more than half the time they confide in others," rather than confiding to close family and friends. As one would predict, his studies show that the closer someone is to you, the easier it is to fear inaccurate judgment and unwarranted isolation, shame, or unkindness.[95] In some instances, the best audience with a little distance may be a therapist who can offer unbiased insight and feedback. Just remember, finding a counselor can be like finding the right medication. Sometimes, the first effort brings relief, but sometimes you have to try several before you find the one that works.

1. *Test the water.* It's okay to dip your toe into the water when confiding. Telling someone you are going through a difficult time, that you feel stuck, or that you don't even know what you're going through but you don't feel right, are good ways to begin. When you decide to dip your toe into the waters of authenticity, your story can start as a tiny ripple. It took me years to use the words "postpartum OCD." I began slowly, then as I felt more comfortable, my self-acceptance grew, my shame decreased, and I was able to share more of my story.

• *Answer "Why?"* Why share your story? Why now? My answer to those questions was that I was tired of living in secrecy and shame, and I wanted to help others who might be feeling this way. Your answer may be that you feel something is holding you back in certain areas of your life. Remember:

REMEMBER: YOU CAN ONLY CONTROL THE HOW AND WHO—HOW YOU SHARE YOUR STORY AND WHO YOU SHARE IT WITH. IT'S "WHAT"—THE OUTCOME—THAT'S THE UNPREDICTABLE PART.

you can only control the how and who—*how* you share your story and *who* you share it with. It's "what"—the outcome—that's the unpredictable part. As Small's research shows, fear of blowback, judgment, and unkindness are legitimate. If what you are looking for is acceptance, then perhaps you need to find space in your heart for self-acceptance before you seek acceptance from someone else.

ENHANCE CONNECTION BY LISTENING WITH TWO EARS

We've been talking about how to connect with others when you're the one reaching out. But what if you're the one on the receiving end of vulnerability from a friend or loved one? What if you are the person someone is seeking to engage in a meaningful conversation?

The term "active listening" was coined in 1956 by Carl R. Rogers, one of the most influential psychologists of the 20th century. Sometimes the term feels overused and possibly misunderstood. But here's the way Rogers explained it himself: "I hear the words, the thoughts, the feeling tones, the personal meaning, even the meaning that is below the conscious intent of the speaker. Sometimes too, in a message which superficially is not very important, I hear a deep human cry that lies buried and unknown far below the surface of the person. So I have learned to ask myself, can I hear the sounds and sense the shape of this other person's inner world? Can I resonate to what he is saying so deeply that I sense the meanings he is afraid of, yet would like to communicate, as well as those he knows?"[96]

TELLING SOMEONE YOU ARE GOING THROUGH A DIFFICULT TIME, THAT YOU FEEL STUCK, OR THAT YOU DON'T EVEN KNOW WHAT YOU'RE GOING THROUGH BUT YOU DON'T FEEL RIGHT, ARE GOOD WAYS TO BEGIN.

Active listening should be a beautiful fusion of validation and empathy. It is in the space between what the person says and what they actually mean that an active listener finds treasure. Once again, genuine curiosity is the anchor point here. Gathering information, paraphrasing to demonstrate understanding, and reflecting back to the speaker to seek clarification are all key components of active listening. Rogers also stressed three important principles to apply to effective listening: empathy, genuine interest and concern, and positive regard for the speaker. In other words, don't listen with one ear while your other ear is listening to your own thoughts, preparing a response. Give your full attention to listening, seeking understanding.

Here are some things to remember when you're establishing a connection by listening with both ears:

1. **Remember these three words:** *"It sounds like..."* These words imply no criticism. They give the message that you have been listening. They also help you to work together to interpret the deeper meaning in the conversation.

2. **Silence is okay.** It's human nature to want to fill all possible gaps in a conversation. And the easiest thing to fill them with is our own personal stories or anecdotes. (See shift or support response, above.) So don't rush to fill the gaps; don't fear silence. Silence allows space. Like shaking a winter snow globe and waiting for the flakes to float down, silence allows feelings to settle down and may induce calmness or foster deeper thinking.

3. *Don't be a fixer.* When someone presents us with a problem, most of us immediately try to fix it. For example:

   • Someone's marriage is in shambles? Don't worry! I can recommend a great marriage counselor!

- A colleague's child has a medical condition? No problem! My neighbor's distant relative's son might have had a similar condition. I can introduce you!

These examples are a little extreme, but don't they sound familiar? Although it may be noble to offer ideas and present solutions, one of the most untrue assumptions is that the person who came to you did so looking for a solution. Most of the time, this isn't the case. They came to you looking for support, validation, acknowledgement, and connection. You should never allow yourself to feel that by *not* providing an instant fix that somehow you are letting them down. The best thing you can do is listen without distractions, read between the lines and under the depths of their issues. Then, after listening with both ears, you'll be in a better position to ask them what they need right now.

> YOU SHOULD NEVER ALLOW YOURSELF TO FEEL THAT BY NOT PROVIDING AN INSTANT FIX THAT SOMEHOW YOU ARE LETTING THEM DOWN.

THE NEED TO CONNECT

"A deep sense of love and belonging is an irresistible need of all people. We are biologically, cognitively, physically, and spiritually wired to love, to be loved, and to belong," says Brené Brown, a professor at the University of Houston Graduate College of Social Work.[97]

"We may think we want money, power, fame, beauty, eternal youth, or a new car, but at the root of most of these desires is a need to belong, to be accepted, to connect with others, to be loved. We pride ourselves on our independence, on pulling ourselves up by our own bootstraps, having a successful career and above all not depending on anyone. But, as psychologists from Maslow to Baumeister have repeatedly stressed, the truth of the matter is that a sense of social connection is one of our fundamental human needs."[98]

When we connect, we are better able to communicate our feelings and to ask for help. Australia's Headspace National Youth Mental Health Foundation sums it up well, noting that although conveying your deepest feelings and emotions effectively can be extremely challenging, "when you learn to communicate those feelings, it causes a chain reaction and allows you to build trust and create stronger bonds."[99]

And that can help everyone to feel better!

CHAPTER 9

A JOURNEY, NOT A DESTINATION

FEEL BETTER AS YOU TRAVEL THROUGH LIFE.

I had first thought to title this chapter, "Your action plan to build personal resilience." But that seemed to imply there is a destination. As I have worked through the ideas in this book, one thought has come to me numerous times: Life is about traveling well, not about arriving. Consider this thought from minister Jenkin Lloyd Jones: "Anyone who imagines that bliss is normal is going to waste a lot of time running around shouting that he's been robbed. The fact is most putts don't drop. Most beef is tough. Most children grow up to be just ordinary people. Most successful marriages require a high degree of mutual toleration. Most jobs are more often dull than otherwise. Life is like an old-time rail journey—delays, sidetracks, smoke, dust, cinders, and jolts, interspersed only occasionally by beautiful vistas and thrilling bursts of speed. The trick is to thank the Lord for letting you have the ride."[100]

That's good advice, whatever your convictions or beliefs may be. We all feel better when we become grateful for each day, when we learn to prepare for and deal with the delays, sidetracks, smoke, dust, cinders, and jolts, so that we are prepared to enjoy the beautiful vistas and thrilling bursts of speed when they do come. Then, our job is to let thankfulness fill our hearts and enjoy the ride.

WHAT WE'VE LEARNED

We started this book with the story of me wanting to swim better, and how I finally found the benefits of goggles. Life can be like that, too. It's important to strap on some safety gear before you start to swim. Feeling better is a process similar to adding goggles that help you see more clearly. I hope that as you have read this book, you have felt that it has clarified your vision a little and helped you to see that you can journey through life with greater happiness:

- *Prepare now for when trouble comes.* Get your emotional safety gear ready now. Recognize your inner narrator and your emotional beds. Train your brain to recognize, acknowledge, and assess your emotions and perceptions.
- *Understand the mental health pyramid.* Learn the expectations written on your invisible chalkboard, so that you can make sense of what's going on inside your head. Recog-

nize your emotional triggers, build on your strengths, and understand that your values and goals are affecting your thoughts and behaviors. Use the optimal health pyramid to understand how social, emotional, and physical health work together.

- *Become aware of your perceptions.* Figure out what is or is not within your control. Develop proper perceptions and prepare so that when an event occurs, you can step back, assess, and respond in a way that helps you feel better.

- *Recognize emotions and thoughts for what they are.* Become self-aware and practice self-acknowledgement and self-compassion. Recognize the experts and experiences who influence your expectations. Analyze your emotional beds. Let past success become a springboard for future success. Use viewpointing to see beyond your own emotions.

- *Refrain from labeling emotions as good or bad.* Start to see emotions as clues, not truths. What is your default emotion, and what is your storyline? Learn to overcome fears by recognizing the story your inner narrator repeats to you. Shift the narration so that your inner voice tells you that you are capable of good things.

- *Choose the emotions to analyze or let go.* Look at emotions as a compass. Let them direct your focus to what you care about and value. Use them to improve your social and physical health, stimulate creativity and performance, and reinforce your values. Align what you do with what you care about.

- *Reframe and change the emotions that affect you the most.* Move through the stress response cycle using breathing, exercise and environment, touch, temperature, and time outs, as well as establishing social connections.

- *Communicate your emotions and ask for help.* Build and maintain true connections by switching from shift response to support response. Look for the right time and way to share your story and thoughtfully choose your audience. Enhance connections through active listening.

With that short review, I ask you to consider that if we're talking about finding joy in the journey of life rather than just arriving at a destination, consider what "feel better" really means to you. What *is* your action plan to build personal resilience during the journey?

So much of feeling better is being able to take a step back and gain perspective. It is to become a fly on the wall observing your thoughts, feelings, and behavior.

Remember our discussion about emotional beds? We can all relate to the warmth and security we feel when we're snuggled up under the covers. It's as if the very sheets are calling your name. However, to someone who has never read *Feel Better*, relating a cozy bed to an emotional state we're magnetized toward might seem counterintuitive—not for you though. Now you know what your emotional bed is, what your default emotions are, and what some of your common triggers might be.

Think also as we close on the example of the plastic shrink wrap stretched over a bowl of hot soup. Can you imagine yourself taking a toothpick and poking holes to let the steam vent? That analogy teaches us to start poking holes, or thinking differently, about our internal narratives.

As you continue on the path to feeling better, remember that building emotional health is one of the most underutilized and yet more readily available ways to improve overall mental and physical health. *Feel Better* is not a book about how to avoid painful emotions. Rather, it is about learning to stop fighting with those emotions. It's about learning from them, processing them in a healthy way, and acting on them before they affect you adversely. As you become more aware of your emotions, feelings, and thoughts—as you understand them better—you empower yourself to properly frame your perceptions and take more control.

When you feel better, confidence replaces awkwardness. You know when to acknowledge, when to analyze, and when to simply let things go.

Feeling better is not a destination. It's a pattern of decisions we are willing to make and are capable of making as we journey through life. It's not everything all at once. It's becoming aware of how we handle our emotions, recognizing that we have an internal narrative, and reconciling with ourselves that perhaps one of the most important things we can do is to acknowledge how far we have come.

Sometimes the difference between surviving and thriving is simply permission. So now, give yourself permission to explore ideas without judgment, criticism, or self-deprecation. Give yourself permission to be genuinely curious about the way you react and respond to the world around you.

Give yourself permission to feel better. Why? Because you *are* worth it.

FEELING BETTER IS NOT A DESTINATION. IT'S A PATTERN OF DECISIONS WE ARE WILLING TO MAKE AND ARE CAPABLE OF MAKING AS WE JOURNEY THROUGH LIFE.

ACKNOWLEDGEMENTS

This book would not have been possible without the guidance and support of Adrian Gostick, Tony Gostick, and Natalie Duell. Thank you for helping these words and stories come to life.

To members of my incredible team, Karen Delina and Lesley Mckelvie, thank you for your input, suggestions, and feedback.

Thank you to the dedicated staff and volunteers at the Foundry Abbotsford and Bakerview Centre for Learning; because of you, there is a place for youth to feel safe, seen, and heard.

A heartfelt thanks to Evangeline Ramos for your love, support, encouragement and helping to keep me going during this journey!

Finally and most importantly, thank you to all of the youth whom I have worked with … for trusting me with your stories, for sharing your past with me, and for allowing our team to show you that "You are not a drop in the ocean, you are the entire ocean in a drop" (Rumi).

NOTES

1. Goleman, Daniel. 1995. *Emotional Intelligence: Why It Can Matter More Than IQ.* USA: Bantam Books.
2. Keng, Shiang-Ling. 2011. *Effects of mindfulness on psychological health: a review of empirical studies* 31. 10.1016/j.cpr.2011.04.006.
3. The Science of Emotions: Exploring the Basics of Emotional Psychology (June 27, 2019). Psychology and Counseling News. https://online.uwa.edu/news/emotional-psychology/
4. Samra, J., Baynton, A. (2010). Emotional Triggers. Workplace Strategies for Mental Health. https://www.workplacestrategiesformentalhealth.com/resources/emotional-triggers
5. Chowdhury, Madhuleena R., and William Smith. 2019. "Emotional Regulation: 6 Key Skills to Regulate Emotions." Positive Psychology. https://positivepsychology.com/emotion-regulation/
6. Parker, Toni. n.d. "6 Steps to Mindfully Deal With Difficult Emotions." The Gottman Institute. Accessed March 24, 2024. https://www.gottman.com/blog/6stepstomindfullydealwithdifficultemotions/

7. "6 Ways to Improve Your Emotional Intuition." 2022. Nick Wignall. https://nickwignall.com/6-ways-to-improve-your-emotional-intuition/.

8. Ekman, Paul. 1979. "Facial Expressions of Emotion." Annual Review of Psychology 30. https://doi.org/10.1146/annurev.ps.30.020179.002523.

9. Plutchik, R. (1991). The emotions. University Press of America.

10. Cowen, A. S., & Keltner, D. (2017). Self-report captures 27 distinct categories of emotion bridged by continuous gradients. Proceedings of the National Academy of Sciences, 114(38). https://doi.org/10.1073/pnas.1702247114

11. Salovey, P., & Mayer, J. D. (1990). Emotional Intelligence. Imagination, Cognition and Personality, 9(3), 185-211. https://doi.org/10.2190/DUGG-P24E-52WK-6CDG

12. Goleman, Daniel. 1995. Emotional Intelligence: Why It Can Matter More Than IQ. USA: Bantam Books.

13. Tan, C.-M., Goh, C., Goleman, D., & Kabat-Zinn, J. (2014). Search inside yourself: The unexpected path to achieving success, happiness (and world peace). HarperOne.

14. Bruk, A., School, S., & Bless, H. (2018). Beautiful Mess Effect: Self Other Differences in Evaluation of Showing Vulnerability. Journal of Personality and Social Psychology. 115(2),192-205

15. Bourke, C. Harnessing the Hurdles with Benke Blomkvist. The Track and Field Performance Podcast. 2021. 1hr7min.

16. Morin, A. (2020, August 11). 6 ways to stop worrying about things you can't control. Inc. https://www.inc.com/amy-morin/6-ways-to-stop-worrying-about-things-you-cant-control.html

17. Morin, A. (2017, May 13). *6 ways to stop stressing about things you can't control.* Forbes. https://www.forbes.com/sites/amymorin/2017/05/13/6-ways-to-stop-stressing-about-things-you-cant-control/
18. Dweck, C. S. (2006). *Mindset: The new psychology of success.* Random House.
19. Combs-Brown, S. (2021.). *Our perception is our reality.* LinkedIn. https://www.linkedin.com/pulse/our-perception-reality-suzanne-combs-brown-she-her-hers-
20. Ibid.
21. Flett, G. L. (2018). *The psychology of mattering: Understanding the human need to be significant.* Academic Press
22. Prilleltensky, I., & Prilleltensky, O. (2021). *How people matter: Why it affects health, happiness, love, work, and society.* Cambridge University Press
23. Flett, G. L., & Bohn, M. J. (2020). The Anti-Mattering Scale: Development, psychometric properties, and associations with well-being and distress measures in adolescents and emerging adults. *Journal of Adolescence,* 80, 95-106. https://doi.org/10.1016/j.adolescence.2020.02.002
24. Flett, G. L., Bohn, M. J., & Hewitt, P. L. (2022). The Anti-Mattering Scale: Development, psychometric properties, and associations with well-being and distress measures in adolescents and emerging adults. *International Journal of Stress Studies.* https://cdspress.ca/wp-content/uploads/2022/12/Flett.IJSS_.2022.final_.pdf
25. Kogan, V. (2021, April 22). *Boost your self-confidence with self-acknowledgement.* Forbes. https://www.forbes.com/councils/forbescoachescouncil/2021/04/22/boost-your-self-confidence-with-self-acknowledgement/#:~:text=The%20stronger%20the%20neural%20connection,and%2C%20ultimately%2C%20your%20results.

26. Beck, A. T., & Alford, B. A. (2009). *Depression: Causes and treatment* (2nd ed.). University of Pennsylvania Press

27. Wright, R., & Kinsella, S. (2022). The seduction of a sunny day: How weather biases car buying behavior. *Journal of Consumer Research*, 49(4), 672-689. https://doi.org/10.1093/jcr/ucac018

28. Brown, B. (2021). *Atlas of the heart: Mapping meaningful connection and the language of human experience.* Random House

29. Wittgenstein, L. (1953). *Philosophical investigations* (G. E. M. Anscombe, Trans.). Blackwell. (Original work published 1953)

30. Hoemann, K., Khan, Z., Kamona, N., Dy, J., Barrett, L. F., & Quigley, K. S. (2021). Investigating the relationship between emotional granularity and cardiorespiratory physiological activity in daily life. *Psychophysiology*, 58(9), e13808. https://doi.org/10.1111/psyp.13808

31. Beck, A. T. (1987). Cognitive models of depression. Journal of Cognitive Psychotherapy, 1(1), 5–37

32. Delgado, J. (n.d.). *The true meaning of holding on to something: It is not what you hold on to but why you hold on.* Psychology Spot. Retrieved April 12, 2024, from https://psychology-spot.com/holding-on-to-something-meaning/#google_vignette

33. Neff, K. (2011). *Self-compassion: The proven power of being kind to yourself.* William Morrow Paperbacks

34. My Online Therapy. (2022). *Why self-love is important.* Retrieved January 7, 2024, from https://myonlinetherapy.com/why-self-love-is-important/

35. Neff, K. (2023). Self-compassion: Theory, method, research, and intervention. *Annual Review of Psychology*, 74, 357-385. https://doi.org/10.1146/annurev-psych-012620-022650

36. Ibid.

37. Ibid.

38. Ness Labs. (n.d.). *Self-love: What it is and why it matters.* Retrieved February 8, 2024, from https://nesslabs.com/self-love

39. Chenoweth, K. (2009). *A little bit wicked: Life, love, and faith in stages.* Hyperion

40. Fairbank, R. (2020). *How to process your emotions.* Lifehacker. Retrieved from https://lifehacker.com

41. Ibid.

42. Boyes, A. (2015). *The Anxiety Toolkit: Strategies for Fine-Tuning Your Mind and Moving Past Your Stuck Points.* TarcherPerigee.

43. Ibid.

44. Ibid.

45. Raypole, C. (2021). *Understanding emotional triggers: how to recognize and cope with them.* Healthline. Retrieved from https://healthline.com

46. Ibid.

47. Samra, J., & Banton, M. A. (2019). *Managing emotions in the workplace.* Workplace Strategies for Mental Health. Retrieved from https://workplacestrategiesformentalhealth.com

48. Ibid.

49. Dingfelder, S. F. (2011). *The power of stories.* American Psychological Association. Retrieved from https://apa.org

50. Holmes, J. (2014). *How stories shape identity.* Interview in *Waterloo News.* Retrieved from https://uwaterloo.ca

51. McAdams, D. (2013). *The Redemptive Self: Stories Americans Live By.* Oxford University Press.

52. Dingfelder. *The power of stories.*

53. Symmetry Counseling. (2016). *Emotions: Neither good nor bad.* Retrieved December 17, 2023, from https://symmetrycounseling.com/uncategorized/emotions-neither-good-bad/

54. Bucher, Emily. 2020. "Why it's important to "feel" all of your feelings." The Ohio State University Wexner Medical Center. https://wexnermedical.osu.edu/blog/why-its-important-to-feel-all-of-your-feelings.

55. Cherry, Kendra. 2022. "Why Are Emotions Important?" Verywell Mind. https://www.verywellmind.com/the-purpose-of-emotions-2795181.

56. Ibid.

57. Wiest, B. (2018, May 14). *If you want to master your life, learn to organize your feelings*. Forbes. https://www.forbes.com/sites/briannawiest/2018/05/14/if-you-want-to-master-your-life-learn-to-organize-your-feelings/?sh=1a47d4f1cb0f

58. Ibid.

59. Goudreau, J. (2021, February 8). *How to find meaning when your job feels meaningless*. Harvard Business Review. https://hbr.org/2021/02/how-to-find-meaning-when-your-job-feels-meaningless

60. Christensen, C. M., Allworth, J., & Dillon, K. (2012). *How will you measure your life?* HarperBusiness

61. Ibid.

62. Nagoski, Emily, and Amelia Nagoski. 2020. *Burnout: The Secret to Unlocking the Stress Cycle*. N.p.: Random House Publishing Group

63. Ibid.

64. Wilson, Debra R., Zia Sherrell, and Nicole Washington. n.d. "Anxiety and drawing: How it can help treatment." Medical News Today. Accessed April 12, 2024. https://www.medicalnewstoday.com/articles/anxiety-and-drawing

65. Ibid.

66. Brody, S. (2021). *Feelings don't care about logic.* Shmuel Brody Coaching. Retrieved September 5, 2023, from https://www.shmuelbrodycoaching.com/blog/feelings-dont-care-about-logic

67. Beligon, Stephanie. 2020. "Feeling, emotion and the company they keep: what adjectives reveal about the substantive feeling and emotion." *OpenEdition Journals*

68. Weil, A. (1996). *Breathing: The master key to self-healing.* Random House

69. Harvard Health Publishing. (n.d.). *Understanding the stress response.* Retrieved November 17, 2023, from https://www.health.harvard.edu/staying-healthy/understanding-the-stress-response#:~:text=People%20can%20use%20exercise%20to,also%20helps%20relieve%20muscle%20tension

70. Pittman, M. (2019, May 20). *Stress relief using environmental and lifestyle changes.* Texas A&M Today. https://today.tamu.edu/2019/05/20/stress-relief-using-environmental-and-lifestyle-changes/

71. Ibid.

72. Artigas, Lucina, and Ignacio Jarero. n.d. "The Butterfly Hug Method for Bilateral Stimulation." EMDR Research Foundation. Accessed April 12, 2024. https://emdrfoundation.org/toolkit/butterfly-hug.pdf

73. Rusnak, Kari. 2021. "The Six Second Kiss." The Gottman Institute. Accessed April 10, 2023. https://www.gottman.com/blog/the-six-second-kiss/

74. Alloway, Tracy P. 2022. "What 20 Seconds of Hugging Can Do for You." Psychology Today. https://www.psychologytoday.com/ca/blog/keep-it-in-mind/202201/what-20-seconds-hugging-can-do-you

75. Hof, W. (2017). *The Wim Hof method: Activate your full potential.* HarperCollins

76. Ariely, Dan. 2022. "To Relieve Stress, Try More Stress - WSJ." The Wall Street Journal. https://www.wsj.com/articles/to-relieve-stress-try-more-stress-11652985460

77. Ibid.

78. Holland, K. (2019, July 23). *Adults get to have timeouts, too.* Psychology Today. https://www.psychologytoday.com/ca/blog/stronger-the-broken-places/201907/adults-get-have-timeouts-too

79. Ibid.

80. Rippe, James M., ed. 2019. *Lifestyle Medicine.* N.p.: CRC Press, Taylor & Francis Group.

81. LeWine, Howard E. 2024. "Understanding the stress response." Harvard Health. https://www.health.harvard.edu/staying-healthy/understanding-the-stress-response.

82. Hallowell, E. M. (2001). *Connect: 12 vital ties that open your heart, lengthen your life, and deepen your soul.* Gallery Books

83. Savage, B. M., Lujan, H. L., Thipparthi, R. R., & DiCarlo, S. E. (2017). Humor, laughter, learning, and health! A brief review. *Advances in Physiology Education*, 41(3), 341-347. https://doi.org/10.1152/advan.00030.2017

84. Askenasy, J. J. M. (1987). The functions and dysfunctions of laughter. *Journal of General Psychology*, 114(4), 375-384. https://doi.org/10.1080/00221309.1987.9712544

85. 87. Friedman, Howard S., and Leslie R. Martin. 2012. *The Longevity Project: Surprising Discoveries for Health and Long Life from the Landmark Eight-Decade Study.* N.p.: Penguin Publishing Group

86. "Social Connectedness | CDC." n.d. Centers for Disease Control and Prevention. Accessed February 13, 2024. https://www.cdc.gov/emotional-wellbeing/social-connectedness/index.htm.

87. Friedman. *The Longevity Project: Surprising Discoveries for Health and Long Life from the Landmark Eight-Decade Study.*

88. "The importance of human connection - CMHA National." 2019. Canadian Mental Health Association. https://cmha.ca/news/the-importance-of-human-connection/.

89. Ibid.

90. Derber, C. (2000). *The pursuit of attention: Power and ego in everyday life.* Oxford University Press

91. Ibid.

92. Headlee, Celeste, and Al Gore. 2017. "Why we should all stop saying "I know exactly how you feel" |." TED Ideas. https://ideas.ted.com/why-we-should-all-stop-saying-i-know-exactly-how-you-feel/.

93. Silani, G., Lamm, C., Ruff, C. C., & Singer, T. (2013). Right supramarginal gyrus is crucial to overcome emotional egocentricity bias in social judgments. *The Journal of Neuroscience*, 33(39), 15466–15476. https://doi.org/10.1523/jneurosci.1488-13.2013

94. Abrams, Allison. 2017. "Overcoming the Need to Please." Psychology Today. https://www.psychologytoday.com/intl/blog/nurturing-self-compassion/201710/overcoming-the-need-please

95. Small, Mario L. 2017. *Someone to Talk to.* N.p.: Oxford University Press

96. Rogers, Carl R., and Richard E. Farson. 2015. *Active Listening.* N.p.: Martino Fine Books

97. Brown, B. (2017). *Braving the wilderness: The quest for true belonging and the courage to stand alone.* Random House

98. Ibid.

99. Headspace. (nd). *Communicate your feelings.* Retrieved October 10, 2023, from https://headspace.org.au/explore-topics/for-young-people/communicate-feelings/

100. Goodreads. (n.d.). *Jenkin Lloyd Jones quotes.* Retrieved December 12,2023, from https://www.goodreads.com/author/quotes/1173522.Jenkin_Lloyd_Jones

ABOUT THE AUTHOR

D r. Shahana Alibhai is a TEDx speaker, family physician, and
mental health advocate.

Dr Shahana has been privileged to work with a multitude
of organizations including the University of British Columbia,
Remax, Takeda and Yale University to help the audience gain more
clarity about their mental health. Her client list spans everyone
from those involved in aerospace to those working on the front
lines of education and healthcare, instilling the message that your
emotional health is directly tied to your mental health.

As a lead physician at one of British Columbia's largest youth
health centers, much of Dr. Shahana's career is focused on those
struggling with their mental health.

She volunteers her time speaking about mental health and how
to improve it in developing countries. "Let's Talk Nepal" and other
podcasts are heard internationally.

Dr. Shahana has created an innovative program entitled "Think
Like a Doc," in which she volunteers her time to perform outreach
in various schools, allowing them to play the role of a doctor and
in turn to learn about their physical and mental health.

Her insights are highly sought after and she's been featured
in multiple major media including CTV and Global. She is best

known for her "Emotional Literacy for Better Mental Health" TEDx talk, and as a panelist at International Women's Day.

She has served on the UBC Faculty of Medicine Residency training program and is currently a national accreditor for the College of Canadian Family Physicians.

She is a mother to three rambunctious and energetic boys, Eshaan, Ayaan, and Rahil, and knows firsthand the challenges and complexity of raising a young family. She is married to Dr. Khalid Alibhai, chiropractor and owner of Stuart Chiropractic. The family can often be found hiking, playing sports or doing any activity to burn off some of the boys' boundless energy.

CONTACT INFORMATION:

Email: info@drshahana.com
Website: www.drshahana.com
LinkedIn: linkedin.com/in/shahana-alibhai-rae
Facebook: https://facebook.com/thedrshahana
Instagram: https://www.instagram.com/thedrshahana
YouTube: https://www.youtube.com/@dr.shahana-feelbetter

FEEL BETTER WITH THESE RESOURCES

Want all of the book exercises in one spot?
Download your free Feel Better workbook.
https://drshahana.com/workbook

Take the free Optimal Health Quiz and get
a glimpse into your overall health.
https://drshahana.com/optimal-health-pyramid/

Get your chance to spin the emotional wheel
and start looking out for joy in your day rather
than waiting for life to happen to you.
Join our mental wellness community to support
your journey towards better mental health.
https://drshahana.com/service/subscribe-to-feel-better-newsletter/

Want more? Follow me on my journey to build
emotional clarity and capacity here:
My website is: www.drshahana.com
https://www.youtube.com/@dr.shahana-feelbetter
www.linkedin.com/in/shahana-alibhai-feelbetter
https://www.instagram.com/@thedrshahana

43353931R00120